Read and Succeed:
Comprehension

6

Consultant

Debra J. Housel, M.S.Ed.

SHELL EDUCATION

Contributing Authors

Lisa Greathouse

Stephanie Paris

Publishing Credits

Dona Herweck Rice, *Editor-in-Chief*; Lee Aucoin, *Creative Director*; Don Tran, *Print Production Manager*; Timothy J. Bradley, *Illustration Manager*; Conni Medina, M.A.Ed., *Editorial Director*; Kristy Stark, M.A.Ed., *Editor*; Stephanie Reid, *Cover Designer*; Robin Erickson, *Interior Layout Designer*; Corinne Burton, *M.S.Ed., Publisher*

Copyright 2004 McREL. www.mcrel.org/standards-benchmarks.

Shell Education
5301 Oceanus Drive
Huntington Beach, CA 92649-1030
http://www.shelleducation.com
ISBN 978-1-4258-0729-0
©2010 Shell Educational Publishing, Inc.

Table of Contents

Introduction

Comprehension is the goal of every reading task. The *Read and Succeed: Comprehension* series can help lay the foundation of comprehension skills that are essential for a lifetime of learning. The series was written specifically to provide the purposeful practice students need in order to succeed in reading comprehension. The more students practice, the more confident and capable they can become.

Why You Need This Book

- **It is standards based**. The skill practice pages are aligned to the Mid-continent Research for Education and Learning (McREL) standards. (See page 7.)
- **It has focused lessons**. Each practice page covers a key comprehension skill. Skills are addressed multiple times to provide several opportunities for mastery.
- **It employs advanced organization**. Having students encounter the question page first gives them a "heads up" when they approach the text, thereby enhancing comprehension and promoting critical-thinking abilities.
- **It has appropriate reading levels**. All passages have a grade level calculated based on the Shell Education leveling system, which was developed under the guidance of Dr. Timothy Rasinski, along with the staff at Shell Education.
- **It has an interactive whiteboard-compatible Teacher Resource CD.** This can be used to enhance instruction and support literacy skills.

How to Use This Book

First, determine what sequence will best benefit your students. Work through the book in order (as the skills become progressively more difficult) to cover all key skills. For reinforcement of specific skills, select skills as needed.

Then determine what instructional setting you will use. See below for suggestions for a variety of instructional settings:

Whole-Class or Small-Group Instruction	Independent Practice or Centers	Homework
Read and discuss the Skill Focus. Write the name of the skill on the board.	Create a folder for each student. Include a copy of the selected skill practice page and passage.	Give each student a copy of the selected skill practice page and passage.
Read and discuss responses to each question. Read the text when directed (as a group, in pairs, or individually).	Have students complete the skill practice page. Remind them to begin by reading the Skill Focus and to read the passage when directed.	Have students complete the skill practice page. Remind them to begin by reading the Skill Focus and to read the passage when directed.
Read and discuss the Critical Thinking question. Allow time for discussion before having students write their responses.	Collect the skill practice pages and check students' answers. Or, provide each student with a copy of the answer key (pages 138–149).	Collect the skill practice pages and check students' answers. Or, provide each student with a copy of the answer key (pages 138–149).

Research Support for the Read and Succeed: Comprehension Series

Comprehension is the ability to derive meaning from text. It is critically important not only for the development of children's reading skills but also for students' abilities to obtain a complete education. The National Reading Panel (2000) states that comprehension is an active process that requires an intentional interaction between the reader and the text. A reader must engage in problem-solving thinking processes in order to relate the ideas represented in print to his or her own knowledge and experiences and build mental images to store in memory.

Teaching students to use specific strategies can improve their comprehension. To some degree, readers acquire such strategies informally. However, the National Reading Panel confirmed that explicit instruction in comprehension strategies is highly effective in enhancing understanding. That's why the *Read and Succeed: Comprehension* series was created: to make teaching comprehension strategies simple and time efficient. This book teaches specific strategies students can use to help them understand what they are reading.

Having students know in advance the questions they will be asked helps them to attend to the material. It gives them a focus as they read. It helps them to look for clues and to identify information they will need to remember. But most importantly, it allows them to organize information in their minds, building neural pathways that will be used again and again. Essentially, having a focus as they read teaches children how to think. This is why the skill practice page always appears before the reading passage in *Read and Succeed: Comprehension*.

Teaching a combination of reading comprehension techniques is the most effective approach for instruction. When students use strategies appropriately, they can improve their recall, question answering, question generation, and summarization of texts. Also, used in combination, these techniques can improve results in standardized comprehension tests. Yet teaching reading comprehension strategies to students at all grade levels can be complex. The *Read and Succeed: Comprehension* series was designed to make this process straightforward. Each book contains 65 lessons. Each lesson has a specific focus to concentrate on an important reading skill for a fiction or a nonfiction text. Step by step, students will learn the grade-level-appropriate skills they need to read and understand a wide variety of texts.

Each skill activity is independent; they need not be done in a certain order. However, it is in students' best interest to complete all of the activities. Using the *Read and Succeed: Comprehension* series will save you time and effort while simultaneously providing students with the vital skills needed to achieve 21st century comprehension and critical-thinking skills.

National Institute of Child Health and Human Development. 2000. *Report of the National Reading Panel. Teaching children to read: An evidence-based assessment of the scientific research literature on reading and its implications for reading instruction* (NIH Publication No. 00-4769). Washington, DC: U.S. Government Printing Office.

Standards Correlations

Shell Education is committed to producing educational materials that are research and standards based. In this effort, we have correlated all of our products to the academic standards of all 50 states, the District of Columbia, and the Department of Defense Dependent Schools.

How to Find Standards Correlations

To print a customized correlation report of this product for your state, visit our website at **www.shelleducation.com** and follow the on-screen directions. If you require assistance in printing correlation reports, please contact Customer Service at 1-877-777-3450.

Purpose and Intent of Standards

The No Child Left Behind legislation mandates that all states adopt academic standards that identify the skills students will learn in kindergarten through grade twelve. While many states had already adopted academic standards prior to NCLB, the legislation set requirements to ensure the standards were detailed and comprehensive.

Standards are designed to focus instruction and guide adoption of curricula. Standards are statements that describe the criteria necessary for students to meet specific academic goals. They define the knowledge, skills, and content students should acquire at each level. Standards are also used to develop standardized tests to evaluate students' academic progress.

Teachers are required to demonstrate how their lessons meet state standards. State standards are used in development of all of our products, so educators can be assured they meet the academic requirements of each state.

McREL Compendium

We use the Mid-continent Research for Education and Learning (McREL) Compendium to create standards correlations. Each year, McREL analyzes state standards and revises the compendium. By following this procedure, McREL is able to produce a general compilation of national standards. Each lesson in this product is based on one or more McREL standards. The chart on the following page lists each standard taught in this product and the page numbers for the corresponding lessons.

McREL Correlations Chart

Skills	Skill Focus and Page Numbers
Establishes a purpose for reading	*Set a Purpose*, 16–17, 18–19; *Ask Questions*, 20–21, 22–23
Makes, confirms, and revises predictions; represents abstract information as mental images	*Predict*, 8–9, 10–11; *Visualize*, 32–33, 34–35
Uses context clues to decode unknown words	*Context Clues*, 28–29, 30–31
Uses word reference materials (e.g., glossary) to determine the meaning, pronunciation, and derivations of unknown words	*Glossary*, 134–135, 136–137
Understands elements of plot development	*Conflict and Resolution*, 36–37, 38–39
Understands elements of character development	*Characters*, 40–41, 42–43
Makes connections between characters or events in a literary work and people or events in his or her own life	*Make Connections*, 24–25, 26–27
Understands specific devices an author uses to accomplish his or her purpose	*Literary Devices*, 44–45, 46–47; *Author's Purpose*, 98–99, 100–101
Understands inferred and recurring themes in literature	*Literary Themes*, 48–49, 50–51
Draws conclusions and makes inferences based on explicit and implicit information in texts	*Draw Conclusions*, 110–111, 112–113; *Infer*, 114–115, 116–117
Uses text organizers (e.g., headings, topic and summary sentences, graphic features, typeface, chapter titles) to determine the main ideas and to locate information in a text	*Titles and Headings*, 52–53, 54–55; *Typeface and Captions*, 56–57, 58–59; *Graphics*, 60–61, 62–63; *Topic Sentences*, 64–65, 66–67
Identifies the main idea and supporting details	*Main Idea*, 68–69, 70–71; *Details*, 72–73, 74–75; *Main Idea and Details*, 76–77, 78–79, 80–81
Uses the various parts of a book to locate information (e.g., table of contents, index)	*Table of Contents*, 126–127, 128–129; *Index*, 130–131, 132–133
Summarizes and paraphrases information in texts	*Summarize*, 118–119, 120–121; *Paraphrase*, 122–123, 124–125
Draws on background knowledge and experience to understand and respond to new information	*Prior Knowledge*, 12–13, 14–15
Differentiates between fact and opinion	*Fact and Opinion*, 90–91, 92–93
Understands structural patterns or organization in informational texts (e.g., chronological, logical, or sequential order; compare and contrast; cause and effect; proposition and support)	*Chronological Order*, 82–83, 84–85; *Logical Order*, 86–87, 88–89; *Proposition and Support*, 94–95, 96–97; *Compare and Contrast*, 102–103, 104–105; *Cause and Effect*, 106–107, 108–109

Predict

Look for clues to help you guess what is coming next in the text.

Answer the first two questions *before* you read the text.

1. Look at the title and picture. What sort of "play" do you think this text will be about?

   _____

2. Do you think this will be a true text? Explain.

   _____

   _____

3. Read the text. Does the author present both sides of the story? Explain.

   _____

   _____

4. Reread the last paragraph. What do you predict about Aidan Wolfe's future actions?

   _____

   _____

Critical Thinking

How did your predictions compare with what actually happened in the text?

_____

_____

_____

The Price to Play

Kevin Donnelly loves to play soccer. Not long ago, the New Jersey teen spent all weekend on the soccer field—three games on Saturday and three on Sunday. He's not alone. Forty million kids play organized sports. But it's not just the number of kids playing that's amazing. Parents are spending a lot of money and time on their kids' sports careers. Kevin's parents will pay about $3,000 this year for him to play soccer. This includes club dues, private clinics, summer camps, and travel.

Many parents pay top dollar so that their kids can have the private lessons and the best equipment. Others spend hours driving their kids to games. Has the love of competition gone too far? Or, are the benefits of team sports worth the high costs and intense pressure to win?

Experts say that kids benefit from playing team sports as long as they are having fun. "We know from a lot of research that kids who participate in sports tend to do better academically," says Mark Goldstein. He is a child psychologist at Roosevelt University in Chicago. "It forces them to be more organized with their time and to prioritize better."

Yet pushy parents and harsh coaches can drain all the fun out of playing. Many say that is why 73 percent of kids quit their sports by age 13. "They stop playing because it ceases to be fun, and the pressure put on them by coaches and parents doesn't make it worthwhile," says Fred Engh, a coach and the author of the book *Why Johnny Hates Sports*.

Even worse, injuries from intense competition seem to be on the rise. The Consumer Product Safety Commission reports that four million kids end up in hospital emergency rooms for sports-related injuries each year. Eight million more are treated for medical problems caused by sports.

Still, some kids live for sports. They say that the joy of competition can't be measured in dollars and cents—or runs and goals. "It's my life," says Aidan Wolfe, 10, a soccer player in Portland, Oregon. "I love soccer. If my parents told me I couldn't play anymore, I'd be devastated."

Predict

Look for clues to help you guess what is coming next in the text.

Answer the first two questions *before* you read the text.

1. Describe a time when you wanted to make a good impression on someone. Explain.

   _____

   _____

2. Read the title. Make a prediction as to what the story will be about.

   _____

   _____

3. Read the story. Do you think that Arturo or Charlene have any idea how the other person feels about him or her? Explain.

   _____

   _____

   _____

Critical Thinking

What makes this story humorous?

   _____

   _____

   _____

Double Crush

Charlene thinks: "Oh my goodness, there's Arturo! I always get overwhelmed with nerves around him and then I make a complete idiot of myself! What am I going to do if he says 'Hello' to me? Or, heaven forbid, what if he *doesn't* say 'Hello' to me? Maybe if I turn the corner now, he won't notice me."

Arturo wonders: "What am I going to do when I pass by Charlene? She makes me so nervous every time I see her and then I wind up doing something idiotic! What if she says 'Hello' to me—or even worse, what if she *doesn't* say 'Hello' to me? If I turn aside now, we'll miss each other."

Charlene considers: "Are my teeth clean; is my hair brushed, my outfit attractive, my necklace straight, and my purse coordinated? Should I smile, or pretend I didn't see him, or act like I don't care?"

Arturo asks: "Is my hair disheveled? Maybe if I pretend I have an itch I can run my fingers through it without her noticing. Should I smile, or pretend I don't see her, or act unconcerned?"

Charlene thinks: "What a humiliating disaster of epic proportions! I must have embarrassed him because he looked away right as I smiled at him! I will never ever be able to live this down for as long as I live!"

Arturo realizes: "Either I completely misjudged her, or we just got our wires crossed somehow because she looked away right as I smiled at her. I suppose that means I have nothing left to lose, though, so I might as well just be friendly."

Arturo says, "Hi, Charlene, how're you doing?"

Charlene exhales with relief and pivots slowly to return Arturo's greeting, a grin brightening her face.

Prior Knowledge

Whenever you read, you bring what you already know about the subject to the text. You use this prior knowledge to make sense of the new information you read.

1. Read the title. Write three facts that you already know about birds.

   _____

   _____

   _____

2. Read the text. Have you ever been camping? Tell what you like or dislike about it. If you've never been camping, imagine what you would like or dislike.

   _____

   _____

   _____

3. Do you think the author has found a new hobby? Explain.

   _____

   _____

Critical Thinking

Describe a time when you did something you didn't want to do only to discover you enjoyed it.

_____

_____

_____

Bird Watching

It was the seventh-grade class trip, and I had to go. Otherwise, you'd never catch me hiking through the woods swatting mosquitoes and belting black flies while attempting to "record nature" in my journal.

Ugh! Three days in the wilderness without electricity! MP3 players and cell phones weren't allowed. The bathhouse had just three toilets and a sink barely large enough for a hamster to swim in. The dining hall and a long, snake-infested trail separated the boys' and girls' camps.

On the first day, we did mandatory activities: orienteering, fire building, plant identification, first aid, and shelter building. Camping in my backyard is the closest I'll ever get to camping again. No need to know how to construct a branch-and-twig shelter there. On the second day, we chose our own activities. There was Mountain Biking, Celebrate Thoreau, Bog Jog, and more. I chose Bird Watching. I figured it would include a nice hike and a nicer place to rest. Boy, was I wrong!

A five-mile hike left me with barely a squeeze of hydrocortisone cream. Ducking the underbrush had my hair follicles crying for soap. The climb burned my thighs, and my hamstrings ached. P.E. was easy compared to this. But when we reached the top, I forgot about all my itching and hamburger craving. We were on a cliff of white quartz, streaked with silver. We actually looked down on the pine trees. The clouds were so close they seemed touchable. I had never seen a sky so blue.

I thought a bird was a bird, but again I was wrong. We saw cedar waxwings and ovenbirds. We saw turkey vultures, blue birds, warblers, and woodpeckers. I had seen chickadees, sparrows, cardinals, and goldfinches at our bird feeder. Yet this was the first time I'd ever realized that birds were beautiful.

My journal was full of sketches, information, and poems. I've never been inspired to write a poem before! Our descent was too quick. We talked about the differences among birds—from the songs they sang to the way they looked.

In the bathhouse I heard an ovenbird chirp. I tried to find him, but before I knew it, the dinner gong was clanging. I didn't even have time to shampoo!

The following morning, the buses' horns announced our departure. I felt strangely disappointed and realized that I wasn't ready to go home!

Prior Knowledge

Whenever you read, you bring what you already know about the subject to the text. You use this prior knowledge to make sense of the new information you read.

1. Write two things that you already know about lions.

   _____

   _____

2. Read the title. Who do you think Gamba will be? Explain.

   _____

   _____

3. Read the story. What is the intruder that alarms Gamba? How do you know?

   _____

   _____

   _____

   _____

Critical Thinking

Could you have understood this story without using prior knowledge? Explain.

_____

_____

_____

Intruder in Gamba's Kingdom

Gamba sauntered into the clearing between the shady trees. His pride was lounging lazily in the heat of the day. Everything seemed quiet, but Gamba could not shake the uneasiness that had awakened him. The females were becoming aware of him now. They pretended to snooze, but he could feel their eyes watching his every movement. Gamba paced with a practiced air of nonchalance. He took a deep gulp of air and analyzed it carefully. His sensitive nose detected a troubling whiff of something oily and burning.

Bakari was up now, her ears alert. Soon a low rumbling could be heard. Gamba scanned the horizon and spotted a small puff of dust. It could be an elephant or a zebra, but he knew it was not. Bakari and the other females pushed the cubs under the low brush into a more concealed position. Gamba growled low and with meaning. The males sprang up and padded about the perimeter in a protective formation. There was tension in their stance, but the grace of their movement showed practiced comfort. If there was a need to fight, they were ready.

The rumbling dust-maker drew steadily closer. As it approached, Gamba could occasionally glimpse something puzzling and glinting above the dust, like sunlight on the water hole at midday.

The savannah grew quiet as other animals had sensed the intruder. Everything was still in anticipation. And then, something even more unexpected happened. The thing stopped, turned, and moved away. Bakari snorted and then flopped on the ground as she watched it go. As the others began to emerge, the sounds gradually returned. But Gamba continued to study it until it disappeared into the horizon. This thing might return, and he would need to be ready.

Set a Purpose

Before you read, ask yourself a question about the text based on the pictures or the title. Then read to find the answer. Having a purpose will help you to get more out of what you read.

1. Look at the title and pictures. Write a question that you hope the text will answer.

   _____

   _____

2. Read the text. Write two things you learned about the Heimlich maneuver.

   _____

   _____

   _____

3. What information do you wish was included in this passage? Explain.

   _____

   _____

   _____

Critical Thinking

Did the text answer your question? If not, how can you find the answer?

   _____

   _____

   _____

The Heimlich Maneuver

When a piece of food blocks a person's windpipe, it can prevent breathing. This causes the person to choke. When this happens, oxygen can't reach the brain. If the brain goes without oxygen for more than about five minutes, it will die. That's why it's so important to quickly expel the object if a person starts to choke. One way to do this is called the Heimlich (HYM-lick) maneuver. People have saved many lives by performing the Heimlich maneuver.

You may have seen posters describing the Heimlich maneuver hanging on the wall of a restaurant. Learn how to perform the Heimlich maneuver. You may use it one day to save a life.

1. If the choking person is conscious, quickly stand behind him or her. Put both arms around the person's waist. Make sure the person bends forward a little.

2. Place one hand between the victim's belly button and rib cage. Make a fist, with your thumb facing the abdomen, or stomach area.

3. Place your other hand over your fist.

4. Using all your weight, press your open hand into your fist in a sharp upward movement. Push your fist hard against the victim's abdomen.

5. If the object isn't ejected from the windpipe, repeat the procedure.

6. To perform the Heimlich maneuver on yourself, put your own fist above your belly button and place your other hand over your fist. Lean over a chair or countertop and use it as a lever to help drive your fist into your abdomen. Again, your fist must move upward.

7. After the object is expelled, have the victim lie down. Get medical help. Even if the victim seems fine, a doctor should examine him or her.

On another person

On yourself

ILLUSTRATIONS BY RICK NEASE

Set a Purpose

Before you read, ask yourself a question about the text based on the pictures or the title. Then read to find the answer. Having a purpose will help you to get more out of what you read.

1. Look at the title. What is unusual about it?

_____

_____

2. Look at the photograph. What do you think this story will be about?

_____

_____

3. Read the story. Write two things you learned about Jonathan.

_____

_____

4. Did you understand the title better after you'd read the story? Explain.

_____

_____

Critical Thinking

Did the text leave you wondering? Explain.

_____

_____

_____

Mysteriously Mundane

Jonathan checked his watch and was pleased to notice he was exactly on time. Removing his hat, he stepped into the shop and glanced around. The place was old and somewhat worn, but had a good comfortable feeling. His hat, on the other hand, had definitely seen better days. There was a hole in it large enough to put his finger through.

Stepping into the room, Jonathan glanced around to make sure he didn't recognize anyone. He hadn't expected to, but it never hurt to double check. He proceeded to the table and selected a magazine at random, flipping quickly through it and stopping briefly to look at the pictures. After a minute he found one he liked and tucked the magazine under his arm, keeping a finger in place as a bookmark.

"This one," he said, showing the picture he had selected to the barber. The barber smiled and showed him to a chair. Jonathan settled in and let the barber put the cloth around his neck. After a moment, the rhythmic snipping of hair started. Large chunks of dark locks began drifting to the floor.

Glancing down at the growing pile, the barber commented, "That's a lot of hair."

"Good. I need a whole new look," Jonathan replied. Soon the barber finished. Jonathan glanced at the mirror and noted that he did look very different from when he had arrived. Just then, a man in dark clothing appeared outside the glass door.

"Looks like your ride is here," the barber indicated.

Jonathan handed the barber payment that included a generous tip for his skillful work. Then he passed through the shop door and joined the man. They had somewhere important to go.

Ask Questions

Before you read, ask yourself, "What questions do I have about this topic? What do I hope to learn?" Then, as you read, look for the answers.

1. Look at the title and pictures. Turn the title into a question and write it below.

   _____

   _____

2. Look at the title and pictures. Write a question that you hope the text will answer.

   _____

   _____

3. Read the text. Write two facts you learned about the Great Pacific Garbage Patch.

   _____

   _____

   _____

Critical Thinking

Did the text answer your question? If not, how can you find the answer?

_____

_____

_____

THE GREAT PACIFIC GARBAGE PATCH

What is the Great Pacific Garbage Patch?

Floating just under the surface of the water between the California coast and Hawaii is the Great Pacific Garbage Patch. This is a huge accumulation of plastics and other waste that has been pushed by the sea's currents into one enormous mass. Estimates of its size vary. Some scientists believe it is twice the size of Texas, while others claim it may be twice the size of the continental United States! It is like a chunky soup, slowly swirling around in the water, decaying and releasing chemicals into the ocean. As you might guess, this is not beneficial to the wildlife there. It is also not good for us.

Where did it come from?

All of the trash in the Great Pacific Garbage Patch came from human beings. It is comprised of things that washed down storm drains, dropped into rivers, or were dumped into the ocean. Most of the waste in the patch has been broken into tiny pieces, but there are things as large as refrigerators floating around out there.

What can we do to lessen the problem?

No one knows how to clean up the patch, but we do know how to prevent it from getting bigger. Clearly, people need to do a better job disposing of waste. First, make sure that all of your trash gets thrown away in the proper receptacles. Litter can eventually find its way to the ocean. Next, make sure that you are following the Three Rs: reduce, reuse, and recycle. The less material that goes into the waste stream to begin with, the less chance that it can find its way into the Great Pacific Garbage Patch.

Ask Questions

Before you read, ask yourself, "What questions do I have about this topic? What do I hope to learn?" Then, as you read, look for the answers.

1. Look at the title and picture. Turn the title into a question and write it below.

   _____

2. Write a question that you hope the text will answer.

   _____

3. Read the text. Write two facts from it about John Barry's time as a naval leader.

   _____

   _____

4. Why is it important to learn about John Barry? Explain.

   _____

   _____

   _____

   _____

Critical Thinking

Did the text answer your question? If not, how can you find the answer?

_____

_____

_____

John Barry, Father of the American Navy

John Barry was born in Ireland in 1745. At the age of 15, he sneaked aboard a ship. It was bound for the American colonies. The ship took him to the capital city. At that time, it was Philadelphia, Pennsylvania. As Barry stepped off the ship, he had no idea that he would become one of America's important historical figures.

Barry grew to be over six feet tall. During his time as a sea captain, he had a reputation for his fairness and bravery. He had strict rules for his crew, including no liquor on the ship.

When the Revolutionary War began, Barry discovered a British plot. The British wanted to block the Delaware River and seize every ship bound to or from Philadelphia. The idea was to starve the American colonists. Barry worked quickly to change merchant ships into war ships. Then he fought the British from a tiny ship. He managed to keep them from getting control of the Delaware River. After his ship sank, he set up his guns on shore. From there he joined in the battles of Trenton and Princeton. Then Barry commanded the *Lexington*. He captured the *HMS Edward*. It was the first British ship taken in combat.

After the War ended, Barry convinced the U.S. government that it should have a standing navy. It was the best way to protect its long coastline. He was made captain of the first U.S. Navy in 1794. He personally trained many men. They served in the navy during the War of 1812. He also trained the men who defeated the Barbary Coast pirates.

Barry left no children when he died in 1803. However, he is called a father. He is the "Father of the American Navy."

Make Connections

When you read, try to think of a situation in your own life that is similar.

1. Tell about a time when you were learning a new skill.

   _____

   _____

2. Did you pick up the skill right away or did you have to try over and over for a long time? Explain.

   _____

   _____

3. Read the story. Why is the ending a surprise?

   _____

   _____

4. How did your understanding of William change from the beginning of the story?

   _____

   _____

Critical Thinking

How did making connections to your own life help you to understand the boys' mindset in this story?

_____

_____

_____

Alpine Competition

William leaned forward on his skis. The crowd hushed as the Olympic countdown clock ticked backward, and then the three warning tones sounded, "beep, beep, BEEP!" William pushed off with a giant shove of his poles. He was enjoying a better start than he ever had before! The wind burned his face as he zoomed down the hill, dodging this way and that to avoid obstacles. He confidently picked the most efficient path and could hear the roar of the crowd cheering him.

Suddenly, William saw a bright yellow blur out of the corner of his eye. Marcus, his chief competitor, was gaining on him! William used every trick he knew to increase his velocity. He had been preparing for this race his entire life. There was no way he was going to let Marcus snatch victory from him! It was going to be a hair's breadth finish, but William was determined to maintain his lead.

Just then, the unthinkable happened! William's pole caught on an icy patch of snow, his ski slipped out from under him, and he went tumbling into a fluffy snowdrift! Trying to avoid a collision, Marcus, too, wound up in an awkward heap, panting in the snow! The two young men lay stunned momentarily and then began to laugh and laugh.

Their instructor skied up beside them, saying, "Well, guys, that is not the usual method of reaching the bottom of the bunny hill, but I guess from your laughing that you both survived."

"That was amazingly, stupendously brilliant!" shouted William, giving his best friend Marcus a high five. Marcus returned William's grin. "Let's race again, only this time, let's pretend we are being chased by international spies." The two happy skiers charged off for the ski lift, eager to begin their next adventure.

Make Connections

When you read, try to think of a situation in your own life that is similar.

1. What do you already know about skiing?

   _____

   _____

2. Which of these sports are you most familiar with: bull riding, NASCAR, motocross, or roller derby?

   _____

   Do you enjoy watching this sport? Explain why or why not.

   _____

   _____

3. Read the text. Does ski cross sound like an interesting sport? Explain why or why not.

   _____

   _____

Critical Thinking

How did the questions you answered before you read this text help you to understand ski cross?

_____

_____

_____

Ski Cross

The 2010 Winter Olympics in Vancouver, British Columbia, marked the debut of a new Olympic sport: ski cross. Ski cross has been a favorite for years at the Winter X Games, which are the Olympics for extreme action sports. Those who compete in it have to be brave—and maybe a little crazy, too!

The sport's inclusion in the Olympics is controversial. Ski cross is super fast and is considered by some to be extremely dangerous. Skiers come out of the gates four at a time and compete for space on a narrow half-mile course with lots of twists and turns. The athletes jockey for position as they zoom down the mountain at speeds of up to 50 miles per hour (80 kph), over bumps and jumps along the way.

Ski cross racers are not allowed to pull or push each other. Even so, this is one tough sport. The skiers all start together and race in a group. They always jostle and bump as they struggle to pass each other. Sometimes they even knock into each other in midair as they go over jumps! Accidents happen, so the skiers must wear helmets to protect their heads.

While exciting, many Olympic skiers fear the sport is too hazardous. Injuries are common. But many Olympic skiers are excited to participate. Skier Daron Rahlves has described the sport as a cross between motocross, NASCAR, and bull riding. And skier Caitlin Ciccone has compared it to "roller derby on skis."

Context Clues

If you come to a new word that you do not know, reread the sentence in which it is found. If that doesn't work, keep reading. Information after the word may give you a clue as to what it means.

1. Read the text. What does the word *ominous* mean?

   _____

   How do you know?

   _____

2. What does the word *transfixed* mean?

   _____

   How do you know?

   _____

3. What is another word for *barren*?

   _____

   How do you know?

   _____

Critical Thinking

How does using context clues help you to read more difficult texts?

   _____

   _____

   _____

BIRTH OF AN ISLAND

New islands are "born" infrequently. Yet one may be created when a volcano erupts on the ocean's floor. The lava cools and builds up. The volcano continues to erupt over time, and the mound keeps growing. When the volcano gets tall enough, it emerges through the sea's surface.

In 1963, a crew on a fishing boat was present when an island was born. Early one morning, the boat was sailing near the coast of Iceland. The men smelled a strange sulfurous odor like rotten eggs. They looked all over the ship but could not find the source of the smell. Suddenly, the boat began rocking back and forth. The calm sea suddenly began to rage, spitting out billows of dark, **ominous** smoke. The terrified crew moved their vessel to safety and then stood **transfixed** at its rails: a volcano was erupting right in front of them!

The volcano spit rock and lava into the air. It looked like the sky was raining rocks. The volcano erupted for days. Finally, the fires were extinguished by the sea's cold waves. When the lava on top of the volcano cooled, a new island sat where only water had been before.

Scientists were very excited because they had never seen a brand-new island. The scientists named the new island Surtsey, after the Icelandic god of fire. Of course, the new island did not look much like other islands. It was only a pile of **barren** black rock without any plants or animals on it. Scientists wondered how life would come to an empty island. They set up cameras. They watched and waited. Finally, after many months, a single plant began growing on the rocks. Scientists discovered that the birds that had landed on the island had dropped seeds that had become trapped in their feathers and claws.

About 50 years have passed. Many plants and birds reside on Surtsey. However, humans cannot go there—except for the few privileged scientists who have been chosen to watch the ecosystem develop.

Context Clues

If you come to a new word that you do not know, reread the sentence in which it is found. If that doesn't work, keep reading. Information after the word may give you a clue as to what it means.

1. Read the text. What does the word *version* mean?

   _____

   How do you know?

   _____

2. What does the word *consumed* mean?

   _____

   How do you know?

   _____

3. What does the word *dissipate* mean?

   _____

   How do you know?

   _____

Critical Thinking

How did using context clues help you to read this text?

_____

_____

_____

ARE WOOLLY MAMMOTHS AND ELEPHANTS THE SAME?

The woolly mammoth roamed Earth beginning about 2 million years ago and ending 9,000 years ago. We know that elephants are related to mammoths and are similar to them in many ways. But are they the same species? Is the elephant just a more highly evolved **version** of the mammoth?

Let's consider the evidence. Like elephants, mammoths were herbivores. Mammoths **consumed** up to 600 pounds (272 km) of plant matter every day, just as today's elephants do. And, just as you may have seen elephants do, mammoths used their trunks to grasp food and to drink water. The mammoth's trunk was not quite as long as the African elephant's trunk. It was more like the size of the Asian elephant's trunk. Although mammoths had big ears, they were not nearly as large as those of today's elephants. Elephants need huge ears to **dissipate** body heat and stay cool.

Both male and female mammoths had huge tusks that curved outward. Male and female African elephants also have long tusks, although they curve upward. However, female Asian elephants don't have any tusks at all, and the males have shorter tusks than their African cousins do.

The biggest difference between the elephant and mammoth is hair. Mammoths lived during the last ice age, so they had thick fur to keep them warm. The African elephant lives in a hot, dry area. The Asian elephant lives in a warm, moist area. Since elephants need to stay cool rather than keep warm, sparse hair covers their bodies.

Taking all these factors into account, it's easy to see why scientists have concluded that elephants and mammoths are different species.

Woolly Mammoths

African Elephant

Asian Elephant

Visualize

When you visualize, you form mental images based on what you read. It is like making a movie in your mind.

1. Read the first paragraph. Draw the picture you made in your mind about this paragraph.

2. Read the second paragraph. Draw the picture you made in your mind about this paragraph.

3. Read the third paragraph. Draw the picture you made in your mind about this paragraph.

Critical Thinking

How does making pictures in your mind help you to enjoy what you read?

_____

_____

_____

My Noisy Alarm Clock

I awoke to the sound of the alarm ringing. The clock was across the room on my dresser. I stood up beside my bed, lifted my arms above my head, and yawned. Then I made my way over to the alarm and reached for it. Suddenly, I realized that both of my hands felt tingly. I had no feeling in either hand and realized that I must have had both of my hands folded beneath my body while I slept. Now none of the fingers on either of my hands would move in any direction. I tried hitting the alarm with my heavy hands. The alarm rang on.

I leaned over the alarm and pressed on the button with my nose. My nose didn't fit in the small area. I tried the same with my elbow. It also was too big. I tried sitting on the alarm—no luck. I knocked the alarm onto the floor, then lifted my foot and tried using my toe to poke at the button. Nothing worked. The alarm kept ringing.

I gave up and walked into the kitchen. I could still hear the noise from my alarm. Slowly, the feeling returned to my hands. I raced down the hallway, up the steps, into my bedroom, and pushed on that button. The silence was fabulous. Suddenly, I realized my alarm ringing for so long was even worse than I thought, because it was Saturday. I climbed into bed and hoped I could fall back asleep.

Visualize

When you visualize, you form mental images based on what you read. It is like making a movie in your mind.

1. Read the first two paragraphs. Draw the picture you made in your mind.

2. Read the third and fourth paragraphs. Draw the picture you made in your mind.

3. Read the rest of the story. Draw the picture you made in your mind.

Critical Thinking

How does making pictures in your mind help you to better understand what you read?

_____

_____

_____

Alexander the Great

In 356 B.C., King Philip II of Macedonia and his wife, Olympia, had a son. They named him Alexander. At an early age, it was clear he was a brave, smart boy who showed strong leadership.

One famous tale about him describes a time when Alexander was just 14 years old. King Philip had brought home a horse to add to his stable. When Philip tried to mount the steed, it bucked and reared. The horse instantly threw the king off its back. King Philip decided that the horse was useless and called for it to be taken away.

Alexander was in the crowd, watching from the sidelines. He insisted that the great horse was being wasted. Many people thought that Alexander's remarks were bold because he was only a young boy. But his father, the king, challenged Alexander to tame the horse. The king promised Alexander that he could keep the horse if he was successful.

According to legend, the horse calmed down the moment Alexander got close to him. He patted the stallion's neck and whispered in his ear. The horse let Alexander lead him. Alexander noticed that the horse did not like the sight of his great shadow on the ground. Gently, he turned the horse away from its shadow and was able to swing into the saddle without any trouble.

Alexander rode back to his father. The crowd cheered his victory, and the king gave his son the horse. His father said, "My boy, you must find a kingdom big enough for your ambitions. Macedonia is too small for you."

The horse was proud and loyal, allowing no one but Alexander to ride him. According to legend, the horse would even lower his body to let Alexander mount him more easily. For years, Alexander rode the horse into many battles.

Alexander grew to be a man with special qualities that allowed him to conquer numerous lands and maintain respect as a powerful leader. He is remembered today as Alexander the Great.

A statue of Alexander the Great

Conflict and Resolution

Every story has a plot. The plot has two parts. The first part is a conflict, or problem. The second part is the resolution, which is the way in which the problem gets solved.

1. Read the story. Who are Kenny and Mrs. Melba?

    _____

    _____

2. What is a muse?

    _____

    _____

3. What is Kenny's conflict?

    _____

    _____

4. What is the resolution of the conflict?

    _____

    _____

Critical Thinking

How did Kenny find his muse?

_____

_____

_____

Kenny Finds His Muse

One Friday, Mrs. Melba asked her class to write a story. "Use your imagination!" she urged. "You can write your story about anything." Then she laughed and added, "Let your muse help you." The class had been learning about Greek mythology and the nine daughters of Zeus and Mnemosyne. These women, called the Muses, provided artists with their inspiration.

Kenny felt dismayed. "A story?" he thought. "What could I possibly have to write about? I don't know any stories, and I don't have a muse." The bell rang to announce the end of the school day. All the kids got their backpacks and went home.

The next day, Kenny sat at the family's computer, staring at a blank screen. He tried to think of a story to write for Mrs. Melba. He thought and thought.

"I just don't have a good imagination," he thought to himself. "I cannot think of a single thing to write as a story. Where is my muse when I need her?"

The warm sun was shining through the window, making him drowsy. As Kenny sat there, he nodded off. He put his head down on the computer desk and fell fast asleep. As he slept, Kenny dreamed that an evil scientist had caused him to shrink to the size of a mouse. In his tiny state, Kenny had to find a way to foil the crazy scientist's plans to cover New York City in green slime.

Suddenly, Mike, Kenny's little brother, shook him awake with the words, "Mom says to get up and set the table."

Kenny snapped, "Mike! You woke me up in the middle of a dream! Now I'll never find out what happens." Mike looked unhappy, so Kenny described his dream. Mike thought it was fascinating. Just then, Kenny knew that his muse had helped him while he slept. He would write about the dream and create his own ending.

Conflict and Resolution

Skill Focus

Every story has a plot. The plot has two parts. The first part is a conflict, or problem. The second part is the resolution, which is the way in which the problem gets solved.

1. Read the story. Who is Juanita? Why is she annoyed?

_____

_____

_____

2. What is the conflict in the story?

_____

_____

_____

3. What is the resolution to the conflict?

_____

_____

_____

Critical Thinking

What would you think about a story that had a problem that was solved quickly? Explain.

_____

_____

_____

THE UNDEAD CHIPMUNKS

Juanita was agitated. Her band, The Undead Chipmunks, had gone through three drummers already, and they had their first paying gig coming in a week. Timothy was supposed to have a new guy lined up, but now the guy was late.

"Traffic through the park is pretty rough this time of night," Timothy said and then repeated, "I swear to you, he is *perfect* for our band!"

Just then, the door flew open and in scurried the oddest-looking drummer Juanita had ever seen. He was wearing a pink woolly cap, red boots, and several heavy gold chains against his furry chest. But Juanita didn't notice any of that because the "person" who came through the door was roughly 10 inches tall with huge teeth and whiskers!

"Hey, Timothy, sorry I am so late," he squeaked, "but there was traffic in the tunnel! Just give me a moment, and I'll get set up." Juanita noticed an eerie glow to the creature's eyes.

Juanita pulled Timothy aside and whispered frantically, "Timothy, did you bring us a *real* undead chipmunk to play in the band?"

"No!" Timothy replied indignantly. "And be careful because he is sensitive about that. He lost his tail in a logging accident. He is actually an undead gray squirrel. And the best part is he works for peanuts— literally!"

Juanita would have protested, but her jaw was hanging open and quite useless for the moment.

The diminutive rodent had begun to play, and he was good! Timothy joined in with his guitar and Juanita found herself humming along. Soon, she grabbed the microphone and the three band mates began to jam. This new drummer really was *perfect* for their band!

Characters

When you read a story, it helps to think about each character. Try to picture him or her. What do you expect this character to say or do?

1. Read the title. Name one character that will be in the story.

_____

2. Read the story. Think about the characters. Describe each character's personality in the chart below.

Eagle's Personality	Kite's Personality

3. Which character is more to blame for the unhappy marriage? Explain.

_____

_____

Critical Thinking

What do you think is the moral of this story?

_____

_____

_____

The Eagle and the Kite

One of Aesop's Fables

A kite is a bird with a forked tail; like a vulture, it generally eats only the remains of dead animals. An eagle is supreme in the bird kingdom; it captures and consumes live fish, frogs, small mammals, and other birds.

One day, a female Eagle sat upon a branch, looking extremely sad. A male Kite perched on a nearby bough.

"Why do you look so distressed?" asked the Kite.

"I am unable to find an appropriate mate," the Eagle responded.

"Choose me," replied the Kite, "for I am much stronger than you are."

"Are you capable of capturing adequate prey to support our offspring's appetites in addition to our own?" the Eagle inquired.

"Of course! I frequently catch and feast upon opossums."

The Eagle, impressed by this statement and persuaded by the Kite's further boasting, accepted him as her mate. Immediately after the wedding, the Eagle said, "Now go get us a tender opossum or woodchuck for our wedding feast."

The Kite soared aloft and was gone a long time, at last returning with a squirrel dead so long that it smelled horrible.

"Do you consider this," cried the Eagle, "the fulfillment of your promise to me?'

The Kite replied, "To obtain you as my bride, I would have promised anything."

Characters

When you read a story, it helps to think about each character. Try to picture him or her. What do you expect this character to say or do?

1. Read the title. Predict what the story will be about.

    _____

2. Read the story. What can you tell about Sheila's personality?

    _____

    _____

3. How do the other members of the Chess Club feel about Sheila?

    _____

    _____

4. Do you know anyone like Sheila? If yes, describe the person. (You don't have to give the name.)

    _____

    _____

Critical Thinking

Although Bruno is obviously going to be an interesting character, how does Sheila "steal the show" at the end of the story?

_____

_____

_____

The New Chess Player

Sheila, the Walden Middle School Chess Club's president, was busy checking in the competitors for the Saturday tournament in the school's gym.

"Everyone is accounted for except a new kid named Bruno. He'd better not mess up my schedule!" Sheila was efficient, but not always gracious.

"Maybe he heard your voice and was frightened away!" quipped Marvin. The other chess players chuckled quietly. While they respected Sheila, they could still appreciate a joke at her expense.

Just then, they all heard an unusual sound. It was so loud that the ground vibrated as if someone were using a bass drum as a jackhammer.

"Oh, this is just perfect!" Sheila exclaimed sarcastically. "How are we going to concentrate with that racket?"

Suddenly, a monster strode around the corner! It was very tall with a shock of bright auburn hair on its boulder-like head. Its skin resembled extremely coarse granite and its sharp green teeth sparkled in the sunlight. In a panic, the tournament contestants started to scatter in all directions.

"Stop it this very instant!" Sheila's shrill voice carried above the din. The tumult instantly stopped as the shocked chess players froze.

Clipboard in hand, Sheila marched up to the outlandish creature. She eyed him with the piercing insight of a master game player and said, "Are you Bruno? You are late, and that won't be tolerated in the future. But, since this is your first tournament, I will simply state that your match is with Jackson. You can set up your board in the parking lot, as there isn't enough room for you inside."

The monster nodded passively and moved off to follow Sheila's directions while the other players regained their composure. Sheila smiled tightly to herself; everything was under control.

Literary Devices

Good authors use literary devices to make their writing vivid and detailed. They use similes (comparisons using like or as), metaphors (other comparisons), hyperbole (exaggeration), and personification (giving human attributes to a nonliving thing). Noticing literary devices when you read will help you to use them in your own writing.

1. Read the story. Write an example of a simile from the story.

   _____

   _____

2. Write an example of a metaphor from the story.

   _____

   _____

3. What can you infer from the last line of this story?

   _____

   _____

   _____

   _____

Critical Thinking

How do literary devices make reading more interesting?

_____

_____

_____

Memories from My Childhood

He came home. As his key turned in the door's lock, his role changed from businessman to father. Our father. We three boys ran up the stairs, four steps behind our dog (who always heard the jingling keys first). He stepped through the door, and we attacked: we leaped into his arms, clutched his legs, and hung like chimpanzees from his tie. This gave him an incentive to quickly untie it and change into "Daddy" clothes, comfortable and comforting.

He became a bridge, and we crawled over and under, fighting for kisses, rejecting the kisses, but wanting more. All his thoughts of meetings, decisions, and deadlines vanished faster than a sneeze.

We clung to him tighter than a barnacle to the hull of a fishing trawler. Yet eventually, the last of us was pried off, and we four "men" stumbled into the kitchen. There, dinner provided time to talk about the day. Dad always asked the questions, and we were eager to share our news and our world with him.

Somehow, he found the time to coach our sports. A whistle, a navy sweatsuit, and a baseball cap were his trademarks. Untied cleats were the only indication that his dressing wasn't done in the team locker room, but at the office.

Usually his cell phone beeped on the car dashboard. At the end of practice or a game, one of us might notice the blinking light and hand Dad the phone. Dad would gruffly respond, "You boys are my business," and return the phone to its spot.

Whether our teams won the game or not, it didn't really matter. We knew we were winners in Dad's eyes. He always told us when he grabbed the three of us in a big bear hug. We squirmed and resisted, but our hearts soared as he whispered, "You're my three-way tie."

What I wouldn't give to hear those words again.

PHOTOS.COM

Literary Devices

Good authors use literary devices to make their writing vivid and detailed. They use similes (comparisons using like *or* as*), metaphors (other comparisons), hyperbole (exaggeration), and personification (giving human attributes to a nonliving thing). Noticing literary devices when you read will help you to use them in your own writing.*

1. Read the story. Write an example of a simile from the story.

   _____

   _____

2. Write an example of a metaphor from the story.

   _____

   _____

3. Write an example of personification from the story.

   _____

   _____

Critical Thinking

Think of another verb that the author could have used to create vivid images. Explain why you chose this verb.

   _____

   _____

   _____

THE WATERSPOUT

It was when the sand started flying up and sandblasting our faces that I began to think that we should have left the beach. Instead, late that afternoon, my dad had stood on the deck of our seashore cottage and laughed as our neighbors packed up their cars and headed inland, out of range of the predicted storm. Challenging the weather to try and dampen our high spirits, my sister, my mom, and I lit a fire on the beach while Dad told jokes and toasted marshmallows.

Now, it was 7:30 p.m., and our laughter evaporated. Our eyes were drawn to the sky, where a dark wall of clouds marched toward us like a solemn, deadly army. The red sunset bled through the storm clouds like tendrils of flames. Below, the black waves of Lake Michigan slammed against each other, pounding the shoreline.

My sister, Kim, spotted it first. It was a waterspout—a tornado with a funnel made of water—and it was heading straight for us! The wind started screaming, and within seconds we were running for the cottage. My mom stopped next to the front door of the tiny clapboard beach cottage. "Where should we go?" She shouted at my dad.

I turned to look at the sky where the waterspout writhed as if it were a living thing in pain. It was obvious that there wasn't enough time to get in the car and drive to safety.

"Under the deck!" my dad yelled. We scrambled beneath the deck, pressing ourselves against the foundation of the cottage, and then watched the approaching waterspout in silent terror. The waterspout shot toward us, as if it were a predator and we were its prey.

My dad shouted, "Hold on!" and something else I couldn't hear over the screeching wind.

The liquid sister to a tornado sprinted over the final stretch of water. An animal eager to make the kill, it lunged over the crashing waves, twisted through the roiling sky, and hit the beach. And then, the waterspout began to disintegrate when it hit land just like a monster in a nightmare when daylight comes. By the time it reached our cottage, it was just a strong gusty wind with raindrops that pelted our bodies. The rest of the storm raged for about 15 minutes and then moved away.

"Next time, we'll go inland to Grandma's. Okay?" my dad said, relief in his eyes. We all agreed that would be a good idea.

Literary Themes

Most stories have a theme, or an idea, that underlie them. The author writes the story to make some sort of point—perhaps about love, friendship, evil, or fear—or just to be humorous and lighthearted. As you read, try to identify the story's theme.

1. Read the story. What is the theme? How do you know?

   _____

   _____

   _____

2. What lesson does the author want the reader to take away from this story?

   _____

   _____

3. How do the emotions of the person telling the story change from the beginning to the end? Explain.

   _____

   _____

Critical Thinking

Tell about a story that you have read that has one of the literary themes listed in the box above.

_____

_____

_____

Cruel Initiation

I think it's a dream come true. The most popular group of girls at summer camp pull me into their cabin and ask me to be "one of them." I dare ask myself, "Why?" After all, I'm neither ugly nor pretty but in that in-between-place of braces and pimples, hair that goes every way but the right way, and clothes that don't fit well. I'm not a brain, but I'm no dummy. I'm as close to average as you can get. Why would the most popular girls at camp seek me out to join them?

The girls go on and on about how beautiful, smart, fun, and adventurous I am. "Wow, they must really like me!" I think to myself, squashing my inner voice that's exclaiming, "Warning! Danger!" After all, average people like me never hear such statements about ourselves.

Each girl takes a turn buttering me up, and then they tell me what an asset I'd be to their "club." My inner voice tries to yell at me, but I ignore it. I've always wanted to be wanted, to be accepted, to be liked and admired, to be super popular—just like these four girls.

"So, will you join us?" the leader asks. I nod without a hint of hesitation. Their giggles should warn me, but I foolishly interpret them as giggles of happiness.

"Well, first, you have to pass the test," one girl announces. I want to inquire why I need to take a test if I'm so wonderful, but I refrain. How difficult could the test be? The first question is easy: Who is Leticia?

"She's my best friend," I answer promptly.

"But she isn't," the tallest girl pauses significantly, "one of *us*." She continues, "Are you *sure* she's your best friend?"

"Yeah, I mean, sure," I mutter. "Er, sometimes." The back of my neck itches, and my sandals feel slippery as I contemplate my response. "I mean . . . I guess not," I choke out.

Suddenly, Leticia throws off a sleeping bag and jumps down from the top bunk. I feel empty inside. My heart and mind spin uncontrollably as my eyes fill with tears. Leticia flashes me a wounded look as she stumbles out of the cabin amidst laughter and vicious cries of "Did you see her face?"

I meet four pairs of wicked eyes filled with a look I can't even describe. Then I rush from Cabin 12 and sprint up the dirt path to Cabin 3, where I hope I can fix what I have broken.

Literary Themes

Most stories have a theme, or an idea, that underlie them. The author writes the story to make some sort of point—perhaps about love, friendship, evil, or fear—or just to be humorous and lighthearted. As you read, try to identify the story's theme.

1. Read the story. What is the theme? How do you know?

   _____

   _____

2. Why did the author write this story—to teach a lesson, to entertain, or to give you information? Explain.

   _____

   _____

3. Do you think the writer will be in another play? Explain.

   _____

   _____

   _____

Critical Thinking

Why does the author use humor to tell this story? Explain.

_____

_____

_____

Toss Me a Line!

It's one of those standard nightmares you hear people talk about. You're on stage in the middle of a play, but you can't remember your lines. Unfortunately for me, this was not a nightmare—this was real. I stood frozen on the long stairway of the set for the musical *Mame*.

That afternoon, Mrs. Hollingsworth, our middle school drama teacher, had rushed up to me—a clumsy linebacker on the school football team. As always, her crazy hair was standing straight up in spikes. She shouted at me, "One of my actors fell ill. He has just one line, and you're the only one who fits his costume! You have to take his place in the opening performance tonight!" She didn't even say please.

I felt sorry for her and mumbled, "Okay." Big mistake.

"Terrific! You won't regret it," she announced. Now, in the middle of the performance, no one regretted it more than she did. On stage, I opened my mouth to speak, but nothing came out.

I knew the scene called for a toast. All the actors had raised their glasses filled with grape juice. Whatever I was supposed to say, I couldn't tell you if my life depended on it. Not only had I forgotten my line, but I also had forgotten how to breathe, swallow, or even blink. And if you wear contact lenses, you know that's bad news.

Doink! The contact lens popped out of my left eye and whizzed toward the audience. In one motion, I tossed aside my glass of grape juice—barely noticing the purple juice splatter on the guy next to me—and plucked the flying lens out of the air.

In the process, my arm accidentally pushed against Andrea Rotelli, the girl starring as Mame. She lost her balance and stumbled down the stairway. She lost a shoe that banged down the steps like a rock. But she was so smooth that by the end of the stumble, she had managed to turn her movements into a little dance. In that moment of panic, all I could wonder was how to keep my contact lens moist so it wouldn't be ruined.

Without thinking, I stepped down to Andrea. I snatched the glass out of her hand and plopped my contact lens in it. She gave me a look that would have driven any actor from the stage, screaming in terror.

"Darling," she hissed at me, a fake smile plastered on her face. "You're so silly! I want to give a toast!" She grabbed her glass back. "To life!" she shrieked, worried I'd interrupt again. And then she drained the juice from the cup—all of it, including my contact lens!

Title and Headings

Always read the title and headings before you read a text. They will tell you what the text will be about.

1. Based on the title, what do you think the text will be about?

   _____

2. How many headings does this text have?

   _____

3. Read the text. Summarize the information beneath each heading in one sentence.

Counting People	_____ _____
Collecting the Census	_____ _____
Using the Data	_____ _____

Critical Thinking

How do the headings make the text easier for you to understand?

_____

_____

_____

The U.S. Census Counts

Counting People

Since ancient times, governments around the world have gathered data about the people who live in their nations. This data is called a *census*. Census data is collected every 10 years in the United States in years that end in a zero.

Census data is important. It lets governments learn about the size of cities and towns so they can plan for roads and social services. Local governments can also decide whether cities need more buses or subway lines.

Collecting the Census

People get their census forms in the mail. They fill them out and mail them back. However, some people do not send back the form. When the forms are not returned, then census workers make phone calls or house visits to collect the data.

Using the Data

Many reports are based on the census data. There are reports on population and housing. There is data on how many students enroll in schools. School planners use census data. They learn about their neighborhoods and cities. They can predict how many students will come to school. This data also tells them when they will need to build new schools.

Rescue workers use census data to estimate how many people may need help in an emergency. They can figure out how many ambulances, emergency medical technicians, fire trucks, and firefighters a town or a county will need.

Title and Headings

Always read the title and headings before you read a text. They will tell you what the text will be about.

Answer the first three questions before reading the text.

1. Based on the title, what do you think the text will be about?

    _____

2. How many headings does the text have?

    _____

3. What can you infer about da Vinci from combining the title with the headings?

    _____

    _____

4. Read the text. Was your inference correct? Explain.

    _____

    _____

    _____

Critical Thinking

Why did the writer use headings to divide this text into sections?

_____

_____

_____

LEONARDO DA VINCI

Leonardo da Vinci was born in Italy on April 15, 1452. From an early age, he had a terrific desire for knowledge. He spent his life trying to discover everything about the world and how it works.

He is best known as a painter. Yet painting was just one of his many talents. Here's a look at just a few things that da Vinci achieved.

Art

Da Vinci created two of the world's most famous paintings: "The Last Supper" and the "Mona Lisa." He painted others, too, but never finished most of them. At the age of 20, he was already such a great artist that he gave art lessons to Michelangelo. (This man later became famous for painting the Sistine Chapel's ceiling.) Da Vinci also left notebooks with sketches of the numerous sculptures he created. None of these sculptures exists today.

Engineering

For 17 years, da Vinci worked as the chief engineer to the ruler of Milan. In this role, he made maps of the region. He designed a system of canals and bridges. During every spare moment, he filled more than 10,000 notebook pages with detailed designs for hundreds of possible inventions. He tried making an airplane 400 years before the Wright brothers did. And nearly 500 years before the first helicopter, he drew one!

Science

Da Vinci was interested in the human body and how it worked. At one point, he cut up corpses so he could learn more. He studied birds, light, and vision. He studied water currents and math. He invented an alarm clock, a power loom, and a steam-powered cannon. He also made a self-propelled wagon, a paddlewheel boat, a gas mask, and a submarine.

Da Vinci always worked alone. Even after becoming one of the most famous men in Italy, he tried to stay out of the public eye. When he died, he thought of himself more as a scientist than an artist. Some say that he had the greatest imagination in history.

Typeface and Captions

A caption is a title or a sentence given for an illustration. Words are set in a typeface. It can be normal, or boldface, or italics. Sometimes words are underlined. When you see text set in one of these ways, it is a special typeface. It means that the word is important.

1. Scan the text. What kinds of typeface (normal, boldface, italics) do you see?

   _____

2. What kinds of words appear in each typeface?

   _____

3. Read the text. Then look at the definitions in the box. Why are these definitions included?

   _____

4. Look at the photograph of the building. How does it help you to understand the text?

   _____

5. Look at the portrait of Washington. What new information does the caption give that was not stated in the text?

   _____

Critical Thinking

Name another word that could have been defined in the text. Explain why you chose it.

_____

_____

_____

The First U.S. President

Washington on one of his favorite horses, Blue Skin

George Washington was an important man in American history. First, he was a hero in the French and Indian War. Next, he led the Continental Army to victory during the American Revolution. Finally, Washington became the first president of America.

George Washington was born in Westmoreland County, Virginia. His father died when George was just 11. So, he moved in with his brother Lawrence. Lawrence owned a large farm in Virginia called Mount Vernon.

At age 16, Washington became a land surveyor. He helped measure and map new towns in western Virginia. When Lawrence died, Washington inherited Mount Vernon. This plantation became his home for many years.

After the Revolutionary War, people knew that Washington was a great leader. They elected him as the first president of the United States. Washington believed the country had to have a strong government to be successful. So, he chose assistants to give him advice. He called this group his *cabinet*.

Washington thought that the *Congress* took too long to make laws. He got so upset that he never went to see Congress again. Instead, he wrote letters to Congress. Today, U.S. presidents still write letters to Congress.

People wanted Washington to be president for a long time. However, he did not want to be a like a king or a dictator, so he stepped down after eight years. Washington moved back to Mount Vernon. He was happy to be home with his wife, Martha. On December 14, 1799, Washington was riding his horse. He became sick with chills and a sore throat and died that night. He is buried at Mount Vernon.

Mount Vernon

cabinet—a group of advisors selected by the president

Congress—a law-making government body made up of both the U.S. Senate and the House of Representatives

Typeface and Captions

A caption is a title or a sentence given for an illustration. Words are set in a typeface. It can be normal, or boldface, or italics. Sometimes words are underlined. When you see text set in one of these ways, it is a special typeface. It means that the word is important.

1. Scan the text. What kinds of typeface (normal, boldface, italics) do you see?

   _____

2. What kinds of words appear in each typeface?

   _____

   _____

3. Read the text. Why did the author put these words in a special typeface?

   _____

   _____

4. Look at the illustration. How do the captions help you to understand the text?

   _____

   _____

Critical Thinking

What is meant by the sentence "That's why there are so many more plankton than polar bears"?

_____

_____

_____

The Interdependence of Life

Green plants are called *producers* in the chain of life. They use carbon dioxide, water, minerals, and sunlight to produce their own food. The food that they produce is a simple form of sugar, which gives them energy to grow. During this process, called *photosynthesis*, the plant releases oxygen and water through its leaves. Producers are important because they not only produce food for themselves but for others as well.

Consumers are the living organisms that get energy from eating others. Animals may eat plants or other animals to obtain energy to maintain life. *Decomposers* are organisms that help break down dead organisms or their parts. Decomposers break down leaves, wood, waste, and dead animals to return nutrients to the soil for use by the plants.

In a community, organisms live together and pass energy on to one another in a *food web*. Food webs are very complex, but the simplest would be a *food chain* such as a plant whose leaves were eaten by an insect, which would then be eaten by a toad. The toad would be eaten by a snake, which would then be eaten by a hawk.

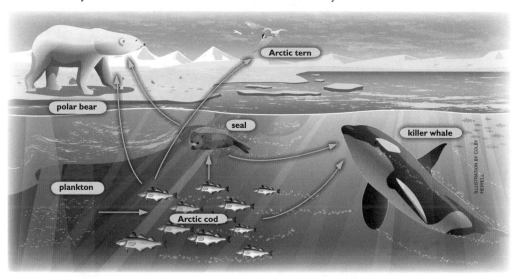

Food Webs

Many, many food chains form a food web. Food webs are complex because a plant or animal in one food chain is usually linked to another food chain. For example, the insect might also be a part of a food chain for a bird, a frog, and a snake.

Energy is reduced at each level of the feeding order. The producers, or green plants, have the most energy. They use some of the energy for themselves. They need the energy to grow and perform photosynthesis. Some of their energy is passed along to others when these plants are eaten. The animal that eats the plant gets energy from this food. The energy can be used to help that animal stay alive and function. The energy that is contained in the animal is passed on to other animals when the animal is eaten. Energy in a food web can be visualized in the form of a pyramid, with the most energy available at the bottom and the least amount of energy at the top of the pyramid. That's why there are so many more plankton than polar bears in the Arctic Ocean.

Graphics

Always look at the pictures, maps, or diagrams before you read the text. They will give you clues as to what the text will be about.

1. Read the text. By what time do the recycling bins need to be on the curb?

   _____

2. On what days are the karate classes held?

   _____

3. If you wanted to try out for Little League, what would you need to bring?

   _____

4. There's information missing about the dog wash. What is it?

   _____

   Whom can you call to find out this information?

   _____

Critical Thinking

Describe a time when you used a message board, flyer, or advertisement to find information.

_____

_____

_____

Community Newsletter

Little League Tryouts

This Saturday afternoon at 1:00. Call Brad at 555-2941 for more information. Bring your own glove.

REMINDER

Recycling pickup day has been changed to Wednesday. Be sure to put your recycling bins on the curb before 8:00 A.M.

Dog Wash in Marlow Park

Bring your dog, and we'll wash it! $5.00 per dog. Flea dip $3 extra.

Call Lisa at 555-0971 for more information.

Karate Classes

Teacher has a black belt in karate.

Eight-week sessions

Two classes weekly, Tues. and Thurs., 6 P.M.

Learn to defend yourself and have fun!

Graphics

Always look at the pictures, maps, or diagrams before you read the text. They will give you clues as to what the text will be about.

1. Look at the title, headings, and graphics. What do you think microbes are?

   _____

2. Read the text. Name three types of microbes mentioned in the text.

   _____ _____ _____

3. Which microbe is shown in the bottom picture?

   _____

4. What does the word *resistance* mean? How do you know?

   _____

   _____

Critical Thinking

Since microbes are microscopic, why do they look big in the graphics?

_____

_____

_____

Disease

We live in a world filled with microbes—microscopic creatures such as viruses, bacteria, and fungi. A spoonful of dirt contains billions of them. From your head to your toes, inside and out, you are home to trillions more of them. Most are harmless, and many are good—they help us digest our food, for example. However, some can make us sick. We call these bad ones *germs*.

Lurking Germs

Germs enter our bodies through our noses, mouths, or other openings. They may also enter through a cut in our skin. A single sneeze can propel millions of germs into the air. Hands that cover a cough deposit germs on desks, doorknobs, and computer keyboards.

Diseases spread in many ways. We can become ill from germs in food that hasn't been handled or cooked properly. Water can be contaminated with germs—such as protozoa—especially in poor countries without sanitation facilities.

If germs surround us, why aren't we always sick? Most of the time, our bodies fight off germs. At times when you haven't been getting enough sleep or eating right, your resistance—your ability to fight off illness—decreases. Then it becomes easier for germs to mount a sneak attack.

Germs Target Children

Kids, especially little kids, get sick more often than adults. One reason is that they don't keep their hands as clean as grownups do. Also, their bodies have not yet mastered the art of recognizing and fending off germs. The human immune system has the job of fighting germs. As we grow older, this system improves in quickly recognizing and fighting infection. This helps us to become immune to many of the germs that made us sick as children.

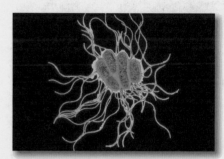

Salmonella is a bacterium that can give you food poisoning or deadly typhoid fever.

Trichophyton, or ringworm, is a fungus that lives on—and eats—your skin.

This protozoan, the entamoeba, hangs out in foul water and the human gut. It causes stomachaches and diarrhea.

Topic Sentences

A topic sentence is one that sums up a paragraph. It is often the first sentence in a paragraph. Sometimes it is the last sentence in a paragraph.

1. Read the text. Write the topic sentence used in the first paragraph.

   _____

   _____

   _____

2. Write the topic sentence used in the second paragraph.

   _____

   _____

3. Write the topic sentence used in the last paragraph.

   _____

   _____

   _____

Critical Thinking

If you read this text to write a report about Vikings, how would making note of the topic sentences help you?

_____

_____

_____

THE VIKINGS

The Vikings were a group of people whose sailors explored the North Atlantic Ocean from A.D. 700 to 1100. They lived in the countries now called Denmark, Norway, and Sweden. Because they lived so close to the sea, they used water as their primary means of travel.

Over the years, the Vikings became expert shipbuilders. They even developed a new way to build ships that allowed them to travel farther by sea than any ship had gone before. How? Their ships were the first to have a keel—a long, narrow piece of wood attached beneath the ship that helped to steer the ship. Even better, it kept the ship from rolling with each wave, allowing it to move faster. Because the ship could get to places more rapidly, it could go much farther without stopping for new supplies of food and water.

The front of a Viking ship curved up into a wooden carving of a dragon's head. This carving helped people identify a Viking ship while it was still far away. Out in the ocean, the ships needed the wind to blow their huge wool sail, but on a river, people rowed the ship. Each ship had 15 to 30 pairs of oars. If the ship was narrow, one man would work two oars; in wider ships, one man worked each oar.

The ships let the Vikings establish trade routes throughout Europe. The Vikings actually discovered North America about 500 years before Columbus did, and they even set up a small settlement in what is now Canada, but it lasted only a few years. Viking ships carried settlers to Greenland and Iceland. Greenland is actually a very icy country, but they called it Greenland to get people to go there. The descendants of the Vikings still inhabit both of these countries.

All Vikings were proud of their ships. In fact, when they died, many rich Viking men and women were buried in ships. Included in each ship were the dead person's belongings, such as jewelry and weapons. The Vikings believed that the ships would endow these people with a safe journey to the land of the dead.

Topic Sentences

A topic sentence is one that sums up a paragraph. It is often the first sentence in a paragraph. Sometimes it is the last sentence in a paragraph.

1. Read the text. Write the topic sentence used in the first paragraph.

   _____

   _____

2. Write the topic sentence used in the fourth paragraph.

   _____

   _____

3. Write the topic sentence used in the last paragraph.

   _____

   _____

Critical Thinking

How will you use what you know about topic sentences the next time you read a nonfiction text?

_____

_____

_____

Florida

Florida's nickname is the Sunshine State. That's because its climate is warm and sunny. It is the southernmost state in the continental United States. Year-round warm weather draws many people to Florida. That's why many older people make their homes there at least part of the year. In fact, about 30 percent of Floridians are over 55 years old.

Since Florida is mostly a peninsula, it has plenty of beaches. Its coastline is 1,350 miles (2,173 km) long. Each year, about 69 million tourists visit Florida's beaches, theme parks, and resorts.

Florida lies close to Latin America. About 17 percent of those living in Florida are Latin Americans. Many immigrants come from Haiti and Jamaica. Others come from Nicaragua and Colombia. The nation of Cuba is just 100 miles (161 km) from Florida. Because of its closeness, Cubans make up one-third of Floridians born outside the United States.

Like many southern states, Florida's climate is good for growing food. Orchards in Florida grow a lot of citrus fruits. The state produces 80 percent of all orange and grapefruit products in the United States. And the state is second only to California in growing vegetables.

Florida's weather isn't always pleasant. The state is often battered by hurricanes. These storms strike during the late summer and fall months. Although these disasters cause lots of damage and often loss of lives, most Floridians accept the risk. For them, the good of living in Florida outweighs the bad.

Main Idea

The main idea is what a text is mostly about. In nonfiction, the main idea is often stated in one sentence. In fiction, the idea is almost never stated in a sentence in the text. You have to read the whole text and then think about what the main idea is.

1. Read the story. Who is the main character in the story?

    _____

2. Where does she work? What is her job?

    _____

    _____

3. Think about the main idea of the story. Write it below.

    The main idea is _____

    _____

    _____

    _____

Critical Thinking

How does finding the main idea of nonfiction differ from finding the main idea of fiction?

_____

_____

_____

The Porpoise Trainer

Marla worked for a sea park that believed its primary function was to care for the animals and its secondary function was to educate the public about them. Most of the animals had been rescued from hazards or illness. Although they had recovered, they were unable to return to the wild. Now they had been trained to perform natural behaviors on command so people could see how amazing they were. The park management hoped that if people were exposed to the animals, they would be more likely to try to protect them in the wild. Marla was very proud to have this job because she felt it was important work.

Marla strode to the water's edge. Thomas stood on the pool deck, watching carefully. Marla had been working with the porpoises for a while, but this was her first day to independently run their training schedule. Thomas was there for safety, but Marla knew that he also wanted to evaluate her interactions with the playful sea mammals. Thomas was her boss.

Flip and Flap immediately swam over happily to greet Marla. She bent down and gently stroked their rubber-like skin before blowing the whistle that signaled the beginning of a training session. Training was straightforward: she blew her whistle, gave a hand signal, or moved a target over the water. Then the porpoises responded with a behavior. When they did the right thing, she tossed each one a fish. When they didn't, she would gently correct them and ask them to try again.

As soon as the training session was over, Thomas handed her a small package. Marla opened it and smiled. It was gummy-fish candy. Apparently, Thomas thought that she had done a fine job.

Main Idea

The main idea is what a text is mostly about. In nonfiction, the main idea is often stated in one sentence. In fiction, the idea is almost never stated in a sentence in the text. You have to read the whole text and then think about what the main idea is.

1. Read the text. Why did the author write this text?

   _____

   _____

2. The focus of this text changes starting with the second paragraph. Explain the change in focus.

   _____

   _____

3. Combine your answers to the first two questions. Write the main idea.

   _____

   _____

   _____

   _____

Critical Thinking

Why is it important to follow the steps of a recipe in order? Explain.

_____

_____

_____

Let's Get Cooking!

Next time you get the urge to ask your mom or dad to make you something to eat, ask instead whether you could make something yourself. Most kids think that cooking is too difficult, yet there are many simple recipes for meals and snacks. However, you have to think ahead. Look up some simple recipes in cookbooks or on the Internet and write down the ingredients you'll need. You can also find a recipe that uses ingredients you already have in your pantry or refrigerator. Wherever you get the recipe, follow the directions exactly as they are given.

Say you'd like an omelet. The only ingredients you really need are eggs. But if you have some vegetables and cheese, then you're really in business!

1. The first step is to crack three eggs, one by one, into a mixing bowl. Sometimes it takes a few tries to learn how to crack an egg so that you won't get any shell inside the bowl.

2. Add two tablespoons of milk and blend.

3. Ask an adult to help you spray a coating of cooking spray or add a little butter to a 10-inch nonstick pan and heat it on medium-high on your stove.

4. Pour the egg mixture into the pan.

5. You can make your omelet healthier if you add vegetables such as chopped peppers, broccoli, or onions to the mixture.

6. Sprinkle a little bit of salt and pepper on the omelet.

7. When the omelet looks like it's almost done, lift an edge with a spatula and tilt the pan so that the runny portion of the eggs runs underneath to cook. Repeat on the opposite side.

8. Sprinkle one-half cup shredded cheese over half of the omelet.

9. Fold the other half over the cheese half.

10. Slide onto a plate, and dig in!

Details

As you read, ask yourself, "What is this text about?" That is the main idea. Then you can find the details that support the main idea.

1. Scan the text. Two students are mentioned. What are their names?

    _____   _____

2. Read the text. What is the main idea?

    _____

    _____

3. Use the details in the text to write answers to the 5 Ws below.

What:	
When:	
Where:	
Who:	
Why:	

Critical Thinking

How do the details in nonfiction text differ from the details in fiction?

_____

_____

_____

Blood Drive at Ellis JHS on January 18

Ellis Junior High School will hold a blood drive on Tuesday, January 18, from 10 A.M. to 2 P.M. in the school's multipurpose room. Staff members from the Blood Donation Center at Cherryville Hospital will run the event. You need to be at least 16 years of age and in good health to donate.

The school's Key Club is sponsoring the event to support seventh-grader Ricky Sharpton, who is battling leukemia.

"Ricky needs our blood donations, and so do hundreds of other people in our community who are suffering from illnesses or injuries," said Jocelyn Ricci, eighth-grade student and Key Club president. "Even though we're too young to donate blood, we will do all we can to bring in our parents and neighbors."

Every person who donates will be entered in a raffle for a pair of movie tickets. The prize is sponsored by the Key Club.

Details

As you read, ask yourself, "What is this text about?" That is the main idea. Then you can find the details that support the main idea.

1. Scan the text. It has the title of a book in italics. What is the name of the book?

   _____

2. Read the text. Write the main idea in the graphic organizer. (It is not stated in the text. You must think of how to word it.)

Main Idea:
Detail:
Detail:
Detail:
Detail:

3. Write four details that support the main idea in the graphic organizer above.

Critical Thinking

How did you decide which details are relevant and which ones are not?

_____

_____

_____

The Story That Caused an Uproar

Harriet Beecher was the daughter of a famous preacher who was against slavery. Harriet was one of 11 children, most of whom followed in their father's footsteps. They also spoke out against slavery. They were abolitionists.

In 1836, Harriet married Calvin Stowe, a professor and an author. He wanted his wife to write books as well. Although Harriet Beecher Stowe wrote many books, she is best known for *Uncle Tom's Cabin*, a book about the lives of two slave families. This story gave momentum to the antislavery cause. It had a greater impact than protests and preaching because people cared about the characters as if they were real people. The book was very popular, especially in the North.

Actually, at first it was not printed as a book. It was a serial, or weekly story, printed for 40 weeks in a newspaper. Each week, eager readers waited for the next installment, or chapter, to be printed. Harriet's story was so popular that it was printed as a book in March 1852. *Uncle Tom's Cabin* soon broke all sales records at that time, selling 50,000 copies by 1857.

However, *Uncle Tom's Cabin* made many Southerners angry. The South relied on slave labor, and the people didn't want that changed. In some Southern states, if a person was caught with the book, he or she might have been put in jail.

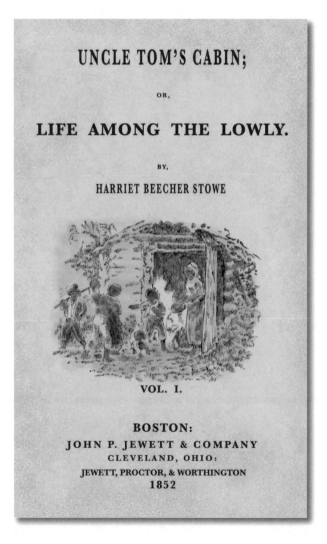

UNCLE TOM'S CABIN;

OR,

LIFE AMONG THE LOWLY.

BY,

HARRIET BEECHER STOWE

VOL. I.

BOSTON:
JOHN P. JEWETT & COMPANY
CLEVELAND, OHIO:
JEWETT, PROCTOR, & WORTHINGTON
1852

Main Idea and Details

When you read, decide what the text is mostly about. That is the main idea. The main idea is supported by details. Some of the details are important. Others are not so important.

1. Read the text. Write the main idea in the center oval below.

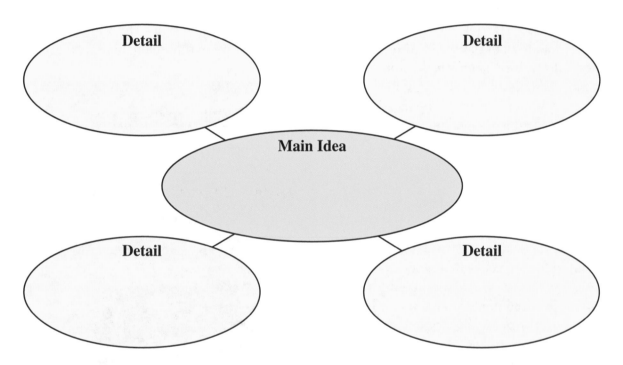

2. Write the four most important details in the remaining ovals above. You can combine details.

Critical Thinking

How did you decide which details to include?

_____

_____

_____

Domesticated Rats

Did you know that domesticated rats make wonderful pets? That may surprise you because many people consider rats to be pests. Some people are even terrified of them, a condition scientists call *muriphobia*. However, rats are very social and intelligent animals. They live in groups and bond with their families. In many ways, their behavior is much like that of a dog! Just as a puppy will bond with a human family, a well-handled rat will accept a human family as its own.

Rats are surprisingly gentle. They rarely bite, and as a result, many experts recommend them as an ideal pet for small children. Most pet rats enjoy cuddling with their humans. They will sit on their owner's lap or shoulder, content to be with their person. Some rats even lick their humans affectionately, just like a dog! Rats learn their names and can even be taught to perform tricks. They love to explore and will romp for hours in a safe location.

Like any pet, rats require responsible owners. Their cages must be cleaned weekly, they must be provided with fresh food and water, and they must be kept in a safe, nondrafty location. Since they are so social, it is best to keep rats in pairs or groups. And, of course, they must be taken out of their cages and handled. If all of this sounds interesting to you, then you might consider a pair of domesticated rats for pets.

Main Idea and Details

When you read, decide what the text is mostly about. That is the main idea. The main idea is supported by details. Some of the details are important. Others are not so important.

1. Read the text. Write the main idea in the center below.

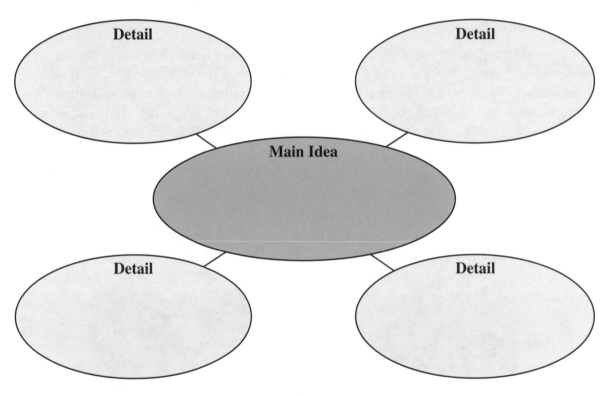

2. Write the four most important details in the remaining ovals above. You can combine details.

Critical Thinking

How did you decide which details are relevant and which ones are not?

_____

_____

_____

Falling Leaves

When we think of autumn, one of the first things to come to mind are leaves falling off trees. If you live in a climate where it turns cool in the fall, you've probably seen leaves turn yellow or orange around October and start to fall. Most people think that it's because of the cold temperatures or that the winds whip the dry leaves off branches.

As it turns out, falling leaves have little to do with the cold or wind. In reality, trees throw off their leaves in the fall. According to Peter Raven, president of the Missouri Botanical Garden and a renowned botanist, it has to do with hormones in deciduous, or leaf-dropping, trees. In the Northern Hemisphere, as the days grow shorter and colder, a hormone is triggered that sends a message to every leaf. It basically says, "Time to go!" Raven says that this causes a thin, bumpy line of cells to form where the leaf stem meets the branch. These tiny cells are designed to act like scissors, and they essentially cut the leaves from the stem.

But why are trees programmed to shed their leaves each fall? Raven explains that they simply aren't needed anymore. During the spring, summer, and early fall, leaves make the food that helps the tree thrive. When the days get shorter and food production slows, the tree knows to get rid of the old leaves before they freeze and die. That way, the tree makes room for new leaves in the spring.

So the next time you see leaves falling from a tree, you'll know that it's just the tree taking care of business!

Main Idea and Details

When you read, decide what the text is mostly about. That is the main idea. The main idea is supported by details. Some of the details are important. Others are not so important.

1. Read the story. Who is the main character?

   _____

2. What is his conflict?

   _____

   _____

3. How is his conflict resolved?

   _____

   _____

4. Combine this information to state a generalized main idea without using the characters' names.

   _____

   _____

Critical Thinking

Do you think it is easier to find the main idea and details in fiction or nonfiction? Explain.

_____

_____

_____

Cousins and Best Friends

Jason was anxious for his cousins to finally arrive. He hadn't seen his Aunt Vanessa and cousins Eddie and Jen in over a year. They used to live in the next neighborhood, and the boys spent time together often. But since his cousins had moved five hours away, it seemed like Jason's mom and dad never wanted to drive that far for a visit. Even though Eddie and Jason texted each other often, Jason was curious about how much his cousin had changed since he last saw him. He wondered if Eddie's personality would be different and whether they would still have as much in common. Jason was a little nervous that they wouldn't have the same kind of connection that they had before.

When the doorbell rang, Jason ran to the door. Eddie walked in first, and Jason almost couldn't believe his eyes. Eddie had probably grown six inches since Jason last saw him. Jason, who was nine months older than Eddie, had always been taller, but now Eddie was at least four inches taller than Jason. His hair was shorter. Jen, who was almost 15, looked much older than Jason had remembered. She was already in high school. Jason noticed she was wearing makeup.

"Hey, dude! Good to see you!" Eddie said as he gave his cousin a bear hug. After Jason said hello to Aunt Vanessa and Jen, the boys ran upstairs to play the new video game Jason had received for his birthday. Jason's mom laughed as she watched the boys race up the stairs.

"Those boys always were inseparable," Aunt Vanessa said. "It's like we never left."

Chronological Order

Putting events in the time order in which they occurred is called chronological order. It gives the events in the order in which they occurred from start to finish. It is a good way to organize what happened in a text.

1. Read the text. On the time line, fill in the important events from Sally Ride's life. (Note: Not all dates are stated in the text. Figure out what must have happened on those dates.)

1978	
1982	
1984	
1986	
1987	

Critical Thinking

Why do authors write events in chronological order?

_____

_____

_____

Sally Ride

It takes special people to be astronauts. These people must be healthy and strong. They must be good at math and science. They must be good problem solvers. These people must want to succeed. And they must also work well with others on a team. One of these special people is Sally Ride.

Sally Ride was born on May 26, 1951, in Los Angeles, California. As a child, she tried many things. She played football and baseball with the boys. She was often the only girl allowed to play. Sally was especially good at tennis. She became a highly ranked tennis player. In high school, she met a teacher who encouraged her to become a scientist.

By college, Sally had two loves: tennis and science. She could have become a pro tennis player, but she chose science instead. She went on to study at Stanford University. There, she read an ad by NASA (National Aeronautics and Space Administration). The agency was looking for young scientists to become astronauts.

Reading that ad was a turning point in Sally's life. More than 8,000 people applied to NASA that year. At age 27, Sally was one of only 35 people chosen. She worked and studied hard while training as an astronaut. The people at NASA respected her. By 1982, all her hard work paid off. She was chosen as a crewmember on the seventh space shuttle flight. Sally Ride was the first U.S. woman in space. On the *Challenger* flight, she operated a robot-like arm. This arm helped the crew work with satellites.

Sally also flew with the 1984 *Challenger* crew. However, tragedy struck in January 1986 when the tenth shuttle mission of the *Challenger* exploded moments after takeoff. All seven crewmembers died. Sally was part of a team that studied the accident. A year after the disaster, she left NASA to work at Stanford University.

Sally Ride working aboard a *Challenger* flight

Sally Ride aimed to be the best she could be and then became it. She is an example to young people around the world to work hard to achieve their dreams.

Chronological Order

Putting events in the time order in which they occurred is called chronological order. It gives the events in the order in which they occurred from start to finish. It is a good way to organize what happened in a text.

1. Read the text. Number the sentences in the correct chronological order from first to last (1–5).

    _____ Abigail met a lawyer named John Adams.

    _____ John Adams was president of the United States.

    _____ John Quincy Adams was president of the United States.

    _____ George Washington was president of the United States.

    _____ Abigail Adams got married.

2. How old was Abigail Adams when she got married? _____

3. Abigail died before her son became president. How old would she have been if she had lived to see him inaugurated?

    _____

Critical Thinking

How did Abigail's determination to learn all she could affect the course of her life?

_____

_____

_____

Abigail Adams

On October 11, 1744, Abigail Smith was born near Boston, Massachusetts. She grew up on her family's farm. Abigail was curious and intelligent. Whenever she had time, she sat by the fire to read books. Her brother went to school, but Abigail could not because she was a girl. In those days, no one considered it important to educate girls. Abigail thought, "That's not fair!" So, she made her own school at home. Her father also taught her many things.

When visitors came to their home, Abigail listened and asked questions. She was eager to learn about the world. She grew to be a clever young woman who was never afraid to tell people what she thought.

As a teenager, Abigail met a lawyer named John Adams. She liked John because he talked to her about important things and treated her as an equal. Sometimes they disagreed about the way things should be, but John always listened to her and considered her opinion. Abigail married him in 1764.

Abigail Adams lived through the events that led to the American Revolution. Her husband, John, was an important leader. He eventually became the second president of the United States. Although she stayed in the background, she helped her husband to make political decisions. Later, their son, John Quincy Adams, became the sixth president of the United States in 1825.

Abigail wrote about her exciting life in many letters. Today, people still read her letters to learn about the past.

Logical Order

Logical order is putting information in an order that makes sense. For example, you would tell what you plan to do on a weekend in the order in which you think you will do it.

1. Read the story. Then put the events in the order in which they will most likely occur from first to last (1–6).

   _____ Grandpa and Randy will fix up Old Blue.

   _____ Randy will drive around in Old Blue.

   _____ Old Blue will go into Freddy's shop for major repairs.

   _____ Randy will get a job.

   _____ Randy will make a list of parts needed.

   _____ Randy will pass his driver's license test.

2. Think of a time when you were looking ahead with excitement and anticipation. Describe your experience.

   _____

   _____

3. What was the hardest part about "keeping your eyes on the prize"?

   _____

Critical Thinking

What do you think will be the hardest part for Randy?

_____

_____

_____

Keep Your Eyes on the Prize

When I was 14, my father bought me an old car that had given its former owner 14 good years. Even though its body was still in pretty good shape, everything else needed work—lots of it. My father reminded me that Grandpa Bill enjoyed tinkering with old cars and suggested that if I asked him nicely, he would probably help me fix her up.

"Randy, you have two years to work on her before you get your driver's license," my father told me. "That'll give you plenty of time to get her running. You'll have to use your own money for parts, though, because I've done all I can just to buy her."

I was excited. Fourteen and I already had my own car! And not just any car; I owned a convertible—the best kind of car in the whole world. Also, I liked the fact that the car and I were born the same year. Well, all right, cars aren't born… they're made, but you know what I mean.

When Grandpa came over the next day, he stood back and gave "Old Blue," the name I'd christened her, a long look. "Well," he rubbed his chin thoughtfully, "It looks good on the outside, but it's what's inside that counts. Let's lift her hood and check her out. You get something to write on, Randy, and I'll tell you what you're going to need."

I ran and got a notebook and pen. When I returned, Grandpa was already putting her up on blocks. "Some of the fixing we can do ourselves, so all it will cost you is parts. But anything major will have to be done at Freddy's garage. It certainly isn't going to be cheap. In fact, you'll need to get a job right away to pay for the parts."

He put his arm around my shoulder. "Randy, whatever the cost or hard work, remember to keep your eyes on the prize. See yourself cruising in the driver's seat in your very own car, and that will keep you motivated. And you know what? Before you know it, you'll be in the front seat, driving around town."

Logical Order

Logical order is putting information in an order that makes sense. For example, you would tell what you plan to do on a weekend in the order in which you think you will do it.

1. Scan the materials list. Can you use soil straight out of your backyard? Explain.

    _____

    _____

2. Read the instructions. Must the steps be done in the order given? Explain.

    _____

    _____

    _____

3. What could happen if you don't put the terrarium where it will get the right amount of light?

    _____

    _____

    _____

Critical Thinking

Which part of making a terrarium is the most difficult to get just right?

_____

_____

_____

Make Your Own Terrarium

You can make your own miniature ecosystem in a terrarium. Inside a terrarium, all conditions are controlled and stay the same. These include humidity, temperature, and soil nutrients. The glass container becomes the ecosystem for the plants within it. Choose plants that have the similar living requirements. This way, they will grow well together inside your terrarium.

Materials

- a glass container (such as an aquarium, fishbowl, or a large jar)
- a cover for the container (such as plastic wrap or glass)
- coarse gravel
- plastic screen or charcoal chips
- soil made up of humus, leaf mold, and potting soil
- plants
- spray bottle (mister)

Steps 1–2

Directions

1. Spread a layer of coarse gravel at the bottom of the container. This will keep water from settling in the soil.

2. Place a plastic screen or layer of charcoal chips on top of the gravel. This will separate the soil from the gravel. Charcoal chips will help to keep the soil clean.

3. Add a thick layer of soil on top of the plastic screen or charcoal chips.

Steps 3–4

4. Place the plants in the soil with a small clump of their own soil. Do not put them too close together. Plants need space to grow.

5. Spray water on the plant leaves with a mister. The soil should be moist but not soggy.

6. Put on the cover and watch the terrarium for a few days to assess the moisture. If it seems too dry, add some mist. If water droplets form on the container, it is too moist. If this happens, wipe off the glass and leave the cover off for two days to dry it out.

7. Place your terrarium where it will get the right amount of light, and don't let it get too hot.

ILLUSTRATIONS BY TIM BRADLEY

Steps 5–7

Fact and Opinion

A fact is something that can be proven. An opinion is what someone thinks. Today is rainy is a fact. You can prove it by stepping outside. Rainy days are wonderful is an opinion. Not everyone would agree!

1. Read the text. Write a fact given by the writer.

    _____

    _____

2. Write the opinion given by Granddad.

    _____

    _____

3. Read each statement below. Write *F* for Fact or *O* for Opinion.

    _____ He treated me as if we had always been together.

    _____ Granddad would bait my hook because I was too squeamish.

    _____ He looked old, just like a granddad should.

    _____ I didn't know about the brick path that led to a private backyard beach.

    _____ Granddad told his favorite stories over and over.

Critical Thinking

Why would you like to meet the author's "new" grandfather?

_____

_____

_____

My New Grandfather

We peeled ourselves out of the station wagon, the hot vinyl leaving imprints on the backs of our legs, and stretched. Finally, we were at my grandmother's new home, just minutes away from a major amusement park!

"You're here to meet your new grandfather. No matter what you think of him, you'd better be nice to him," our parents warned us as my brother and I noticed the oranges in the trees lining the driveway, the lemons and limes in bushel baskets near the front door, and softball-size grapefruits dangling from the branches.

My grandmother met us at the front door, as did my new grandfather. I rapidly analyzed my new granddad. He didn't look new. He looked old, just like a granddad should. When he hugged me, his arms were strong. Plus, he whispered, "I bet you can't wait to ride the roller coasters!" He knew the real reason we had driven for nearly three days.

I smiled. The only thing that felt new about my granddad was his house. I didn't know where we were going to sleep or recognize the fancy chandelier over the dining room table. I had never seen the medals shining behind glass, the camel saddle, or the ivory statues hiding in the ferns. I didn't know about the brick path that led to a private backyard beach or the motorboat docked in the lake.

After several visits, the house became more familiar to me. Now I have many memories of my time there with my new grandfather. We would sit by the lake fishing together, and Granddad would bait my hook because I was too squeamish. He would drive his motorboat and patiently circle around again and again as I fell while learning how to water ski. I remember him telling his favorite stories over and over—about Annapolis, the war, the Purple Heart.

My granddad was never really "new" to me. But he did give me new memories that I will cherish forever— memories of his house on the lake, the fruit trees, and yes, the roller coasters. Most of all, I remember my granddad's love and generosity. Because once long ago, when I was new to him, he treated me as if we had always been together.

Fact and Opinion

A fact is something that can be proven. An opinion is what someone thinks. Today is rainy is a fact. You can prove it by stepping outside. Rainy days are wonderful is an opinion. Not everyone would agree!

1. Read the text. Then read each statement from Robert and his father's conversation. Write *F* for Fact or *O* for Opinion.

    _____ "On very hot days, water vapor in the air may rise to 100 percent."

    _____ "Those kinds of days are awful unless you're in a swimming pool."

    _____ "Relative humidity is given as a percentage."

    _____ "Air is a mixture of gases, mainly oxygen and nitrogen."

    _____ "Someday I'll be watching you give the evening weather report."

2. What does 10 percent relative humidity mean?

    _____

    What would the air feel like at that level of relative humidity?

    _____

Critical Thinking

Should a weather forecast consist of facts, opinions, or both? Explain.

_____

_____

_____

Understanding Relative Humidity

Robert and his father watched the evening news together as the meteorologist gave the local weather report: "Sunrise Friday at 5:37. Sunset at 8:45. Relative humidity at 80 percent and rising. Winds out of the south-southwest at 12 miles per hour. It will be a hot, steamy day tomorrow, folks. Be sure your air conditioner is working."

"What does she mean by relative humidity?" Robert asked his father. "Why is it important? And why did she say it will be hot and steamy because it's rising?"

"Whoa, slow down," said his father, holding up his hand. "Each of those is a question that must be answered one at a time. First, let's deal with relative humidity. Humidity is the amount of water vapor in the air around us. Air is a mixture of gases, mainly oxygen and nitrogen. These gases always stay in the same proportions, but the amount of water vapor they hold can change. Relative humidity is given as a percentage. One hundred percent relative humidity means the air is holding the maximum amount of water vapor it can at that temperature. What does fifty percent relative humidity mean?" His father waited for Robert's answer.

After giving it some thought, Robert replied, "Fifty percent means that the air is holding half of the total water vapor it can hold."

"That's correct," said his father. "Now here's why relative humidity is important. On very hot days, water vapor in the air may rise to 100 percent. If it does, it will cause clouds, fog, or rain. In order to predict which it will be, we must know how much water vapor there is in the air. So…why does rising humidity mean it will be hot and steamy?"

Robert said, "From what you've told me, I think humidity forms when it is hot and water condenses into water vapor in the air. If it is getting close to 100 percent, it means the air is loaded with water vapor and that means it will be hot and steamy. Yuck! Those kinds of days are awful unless you're in a swimming pool."

"You're right about that!" agreed his father. Then he grinned and added, "Someday I'll be watching you give the evening weather report."

Proposition and Support

A proposition is a writer's opinion. The writer wants the reader to agree. So the writer gives support (reasons and information) to get the reader to share the same opinion.

1. Read the title. What do you think the writer's proposition will be?

    _____

2. Read the text. Name three reasons why the writer is worried about national parks.

    _____

    _____

    _____

3. What is one solution that the writer proposes?

    _____

    _____

4. Name two people (or groups) who might protest against the writer's ideas.

    _____

    _____

Critical Thinking

How effective was the writer in persuading you that his or her ideas are good? Explain.

_____

_____

_____

The Daily Trumpet

Saving Our National Parks

Tourist traffic backs up at one of the entrances to Grand Canyon National Park.

There is no more beautiful place in the world than Yellowstone National Park. Except maybe Denali National Park in Alaska. Or Grand Canyon National Park. Or the Fire Island National Seashore. The U.S. national park system is a treasure that must be preserved. The United States is covered from sea to shining sea with cities and highways and factories. The amount of green area shrinks all the time.

National parks are among the few places where nature is protected. They are oases where we can relax and view wildlife in its own element. This allows us to experience what the nation looked like hundreds of years ago, when it was pure and unspoiled. But the U.S. park system is in grave danger.

Too Many Tourists

A glut of tourists chokes the parks with cars that cause pollution and run over wildlife.

At the entrance to Yellowstone Park, rangers have air pumped into their booths because the pollution is so bad!

Many people camp in the parks. Their poorly tended campfires have turned into wildfires, burning thousands of precious acres. Around coastal parks, motorboats harm and scare wildlife, sometimes preventing them from mating. Oil and gas spilling from the boats' motors pollute the water. During the winter, loud snowmobiles destroy the quiet peace of the parks. In addition to noise pollution, they bring air pollution and terrify the animals.

Let's Take Action

The solution is clear. The park service must get tough with tourists. Drastically reduce the number of cars allowed into the parks. Cut the number of snowmobiles or disallow them altogether. Forbid motorboats near coastal parks. Sure, some people will be outraged. However, in the end, they will like the results.

Stop the Sellout

There is another problem that is even more dangerous than tourists. Our park system is being sold piece by piece to the private sector. Some parkland has already been used for development. Soon there may be private housing built on these preserves that were once untouchable. Another catastrophe is opening public lands to oil drilling. Oil drilling can easily damage delicate ecosystems.

We think the U.S. government should keep the parks from being overused and run down. They should also make sure the public lands cannot be sold to private investors. After all, once the parks are gone, we can't get new ones.

Proposition and Support

A proposition is a writer's opinion. The writer wants the reader to agree. So the writer gives support (reasons and information) to get the reader to share the same opinion.

1. Read the title. What do you think the writer's proposition will be?

    _____

2. Read the text. What two nations were involved in the space race?

    _____

3. How does the author feel about space exploration? How do you know?

    _____

    _____

4. Write two supporting details (reasons or facts) for the writer's proposition.

    _____

    _____

5. Name one argument against space exploration.

    _____

Critical Thinking

How would you evaluate the costs of exploring space? Explain.

_____

_____

_____

Fascinated by Space

The space race began in 1957 when the Soviet Union launched *Sputnik 1,* the world's first manmade satellite. Four years later, Soviet cosmonaut Yuri Gagarin became the first person to enter space when he piloted a spacecraft.

In 1969, the *Apollo 11* mission made the United States the first country to put a person on the moon. As astronaut Neil Armstrong stepped onto the moon's surface, he said, "That's one small step for man, one giant leap for mankind."

Today, the largest space research group in the world is the National Aeronautics and Space Administration (NASA). It developed the space shuttle, the only type of spacecraft that can be used repeatedly. Since 1981, the space shuttle fleet has had more than 100 flights.

In 1983, the space probe *Pioneer 10* became the first manmade object to leave the solar system. It had been launched from Earth 11 years earlier.

The International Space Station

Our Space Base

You have probably heard about the wonderful laboratory floating in space. The International Space Station (ISS) is one of the brightest objects in the night sky. Astronauts live there and carry out experiments. There are always at least two people on board. The first crew got there in 2000. Most crew members stay about six months. People from 16 nations have been fortunate enough to work on it.

The Future of Space

What does the future hold for space exploration? NASA's plans for the future will take us to new heights! The next manned trip to the moon is planned for 2018. This mission will last about seven days. There are also plans for astronauts to visit Mars by 2028. This would be a much longer mission. Astronauts could stay on the planet's surface for 500 days. Think of all they could learn in that amount of time.

***New Horizons* lifts off for more space exploration**

Pluto should get a visit from Earth, too. Pluto is a dwarf planet at the edge of the solar system. In January 2006, NASA launched the *New Horizons* spacecraft. It is due to reach Pluto in 2015. This unmanned spacecraft will fly past Pluto and send images and data back to Earth. *New Horizons* is sure to gather important data that will help us learn more about our solar system and the universe.

Author's Purpose

When you read, ask yourself why the author wrote the text. Read carefully to determine the author's view about the topic.

1. Read the text. Why did the author write this text?

   _____

   _____

2. How does the author feel about animal shelters? How do you know?

   _____

   _____

3. Check the number of animals entering shelters last year and the number euthanized. Approximately how many shelter animals found homes?

   _____

4. Why did the author include information about the number of animals that are euthanized?

   _____

   _____

Critical Thinking

Where would you most likely read a text like this? Explain.

_____

_____

_____

Spay or Neuter Your Pet!

Did you know that in the United States for every child born, there are 15 dogs and 45 cats born? Just one out of 10 dogs finds a permanent home. The statistics are even worse for cats: just one out of 12 cats finds a forever home. As a result, there has been a major increase in the number of cats and dogs left at animal shelters around the country. Last year, the Humane Society of the United States estimated that seven million homeless animals entered animal shelters.

Shelters are running out of room to house these pets, which means that many animals are being put to death. Approximately three million cats and dogs are euthanized in shelters every year. While these facts are shocking, you can make a difference in three important ways:

1. Spay or neuter your pet. If your dog or cat is not "fixed," then you could be adding to the number of homeless animals with an unwanted litter.

2. When you want a pet, check out an animal shelter or rescue organization. They have every kind of cat and dog breed. About 25 percent of all animals in rescue are purebreds. Rescue organizations have puppies and kittens and older animals that are already trained. These make wonderful pets—and you'll be saving a life.

3. Consider giving your time or money to your local shelter. Many shelters need volunteers to help care for the animals. Even a donation of a bag of dog or cat food will help.

Author's Purpose

When you read, ask yourself why the author wrote the text. Read carefully to determine the author's view about the topic.

1. Read the text. Why did the author write this text?

   _____

   _____

2. How does the author feel about turtle poachers?

   _____

   _____

3. What benefit did the community discover from protecting the turtles?

   _____

   _____

4. What does the author hope the reader will believe after reading this text?

   _____

   _____

Critical Thinking

How do the guards know which beaches to patrol?

_____

_____

_____

TURNING THE TIDE FOR SEA TURTLES

As evening falls, the light dims on La Escobilla (es-koh-BEE-yuh) Beach in Mexico. Slowly, thousands of sea turtles emerge from the waves. They crawl across the sand on unsteady flippers. Each one is returning to the beach where she hatched many years before. The turtles have come back to lay their eggs.

La Escobilla Beach is a big nesting ground for olive ridley sea turtles. Every year, from June to December, female olive ridleys come ashore to build their nests and lay their eggs. Then they cover the eggs with sand and return to the ocean. After 45 days, the babies hatch and make a fast—and often fatal—dash for the ocean. This has gone on for about 150 million years.

Turtles outlived the dinosaurs, but they're no match for modern problems. Poachers (illegal hunters) kill many turtles. Poachers want their meat and shells, and they also take their eggs. Some turtles get caught in fishing nets. Others are killed by pollution.

Protecting the Turtles

Today, the world's population of sea turtles is way too small. Scientists are worried about two species that live in the Pacific Ocean. They are the loggerhead and leatherback turtles. These species may be extinct in 30 years if nothing is done to help them.

Fortunately, a program in Mexico has shown that the tide can be turned for sea turtles. At the La Escobilla and Morro Ayuta (eye-YOU-tuh) beaches, the olive ridley population has increased. This year, officials expect that there will be one million olive ridley nests at La Escobilla alone. That's four times as many as there were in 1990. That's the year when sea turtle hunting was banned in Mexico.

Now, guards patrol the beaches to protect nesting turtles and their eggs. At the Turtle Center near La Escobilla, kids and adults learn about turtle protection. Although poachers still steal turtles and eggs, most of the community tries to help the animals. The turtle population attracts tourists, bringing much-needed cash to the area. As one community member says, "When the people understand how they benefit from the turtles, they want to help the turtles."

Compare and Contrast

When you compare, you ask yourself how things are the same. When you contrast, you focus on how things are different.

1. Read the text. Then fill in the middle column of the chart below. The first one is done for you.

What to Consider	Your Options	Your Preference
Type of College	two-year or four-year, technical or online	
Size of College		
Where to Live		
College's Surrounding Environment		

2. Fill in the third column of the chart with your own preferences. Just fill it in based on how you feel today.

Critical Thinking

Why is choosing a college such an important decision? Explain.

_____

_____

_____

Choosing a College

Have you thought at all about where you'd like to go to college? There are thousands of colleges and universities. You can attend a two-year community college or a four-year college. There are technical schools or online programs you can attend from home. If you know what kind of career you want to pursue, it makes it easier to narrow down your choices because you'll want to attend a school with a strong program in your field.

Big or Small?

Some colleges have 20,000 or more students. They have hundreds of programs to choose from, and some classes might be held in huge lecture halls. Other schools are on small campuses with fewer than 1,000 students. These kinds of schools have some classes that are smaller than the one you're in now. It's good to know whether you're the kind of student who likes to get to know your teacher or whether it's more important that you have access to a large number of programs and clubs. Are sports important to you? Some schools don't have any sports teams, while others have a long tradition of top football and basketball programs.

Home or Away

Have you thought about whether you'll live at home when you're in college or go away? If you go away, there are even more questions to consider. Some schools are in big cities with lots to do, while others are in quiet, rural settings or even suburban areas. It's important to know what kind of setting fits your personality best.

Time Is on Your Side

There are many college guidebooks and websites that can help you choose. Then you have to have good enough grades to get into your college of choice. Fortunately, you have a long time to think about it before you need to make a choice!

Compare and Contrast

When you compare, you ask yourself how things are the same. When you contrast, you focus on how things are different.

As you read, think about how nonrenewable energy and renewable energy are alike. Notice how they are different.

1. On Venn diagram below, write the facts that apply to nonrenewable energy on the left side. Write the facts that apply to renewable energy on the right side. Write the facts that apply to both kinds of energy in the center.

nonrenewable energy

both

renewable energy

Critical Thinking

Which renewable energy source do you think is the most useful? Why?

_____

_____

_____

MAKING ELECTRICITY

Think of how you used electricity today. Did you cook breakfast in the microwave? Turn on a light? Use a computer? All of these things use electricity. Electricity must be created. Usually this means that a power plant burns gas, oil, or coal to make electricity. These are all fossil fuels. Such fuels formed deep underground over millions of years. First, dead plants and animals rotted. After millions of years and high pressure from the weight of the ground above, they changed into gas, oil, or coal. The world has used fossil fuels for energy for more than 100 years. However, burning them causes pollution, and Earth is running out of them. They are nonrenewable energy sources. Within 40 years, there probably won't be any left. Yet we can't wait a million years for more to form!

Scientists are working to find new ways to get the power we need. They know we urgently need new ways to make electricity. They would prefer to find ways that won't cause pollution. Their hope is to use renewable energy sources such as the sun and the wind. Unlike fossil fuels, they will never run out.

Right now, no one knows the best way to capture the sun's rays and change them into electrical power. There have been some successes. Japan and other nations have constructed houses with solar roof tiles. These tiles collect sunshine even on overcast days. So far, the tiles have worked and have made all of the electricity a family needs each day. Now some cars have been built that use solar tiles to produce part of their energy needs.

For hundreds of years, people in the Netherlands have used windmills for energy. Today's windmills are taller and have lightweight blades to catch more wind. Some have propellers mounted on heads that turn; this allows the windmill to get the most wind possible, no matter which way the wind blows. In parts of the western United States, wind "farms" have hundreds of windmills standing on otherwise unused land. The electricity they generate powers homes and businesses in cities many miles away.

Burning fossil fuels pollutes the air.
SILOTO / SHUTTERSTOCK, INC.

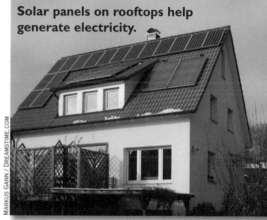
Solar panels on rooftops help generate electricity.
MARKUS GANN / DREAMSTIME.COM

Solar electric cars are cleaner for the environment.
MTOOME / DREAMSTIME.COM

Wind power is a clean way to produce electricity.
PHOTOS.COM

Cause and Effect

A cause makes something else happen. The effect is what happens. When you read, notice cause-and-effect relationships. This will help you to understand how and why things occur.

1. Read the text. What caused the press to give Phil Michaels a nickname?

   _____

   _____

2. Tell what caused Diego to admire Phil Michaels.

   _____

   _____

3. What was the effect on Diego's friends and teachers when he acted like Phil Michaels?

   _____

   _____

4. What caused Diego to stop admiring the baseball player?

   _____

   _____

Critical Thinking

What do you think will be the long-term effect of Phil Michaels's behavior?

_____

_____

_____

Bad Boy Michaels Loses a Fan

Diego Garcia was a sixth-grade boy who liked to play baseball. Anytime he wasn't in class or home doing chores, you could find him on the ball field. Everyone said that someday Diego would be a famous ballplayer.

Diego's idol was an amazing baseball player named Phil Michaels. The sportswriters had nicknamed him "Bad Boy Michaels" because he was always in trouble. He was either in a fight or staying out past the team curfew. On the field, he argued with the umpires or attacked pitchers after accusing them of trying to hit him with a ball. The only reason anyone tolerated his temper and bad attitude was because he was a talented ball player.

Diego considered Bad Boy his idol and wanted to be just like him. He even started calling himself Bad Boy. Just like the baseball player, Diego picked fights with his friends. He got into trouble in school by talking back to the teachers, teasing other students, and getting sent to the principal's office. At home, he was mean to his sisters and brothers, and talked back to his mother when she asked him to do chores. It didn't take long before his teachers, his friends, and even his parents didn't like Bad Boy Garcia very much.

One day, Diego's father asked him if he would like to go to a baseball game. "Phil Michaels is playing, and the assistant coach is my friend. He can get us in so you can meet Bad Boy." Diego was delighted to get a chance to meet his idol in person.

When the big day came, Diego and his dad went to the team's locker room. His dad's friend led them into the room where Bad Boy was talking to the press. Watching the brief press conference, Diego was surprised, although he shouldn't have been. Bad Boy was being rude and impatient in his responses to the questions asked by the reporters. Then Diego's dad's friend introduced them to Bad Boy, who scowled and said,

"Why do you keep bringing these annoying kids to see me? Get lost, brat—can't you see I'm busy?" Diego was so stunned he couldn't even speak. He felt as if he had been slapped in the face.

That day, Phil Michaels lost yet another fan. Diego no longer idolized him. Being mean to people—especially fans—was not the kind of ballplayer he wanted to be. When Diego returned to acting like his normal self, everyone around him breathed a sigh of relief.

Cause and Effect

A cause makes something else happen. The effect is what happens. When you read, notice cause-and-effect relationships. This will help you to understand how and why things occur.

1. Read the text. What causes a roller coaster to follow its track?

   _____

2. What causes a rider to stay inside an upside-down coaster car?

   _____

   _____

3. What is the effect of the brakes on the free-fall ride?

   _____

   _____

4. What is the effect of releasing a roller coaster train at the top of the highest hill?

   _____

   _____

Critical Thinking

Why do people enjoy amusement rides?

_____

_____

_____

AMUSEMENT PARK RIDES

Millions of people visit amusement parks every year, but few people understand how the rides work. For instance, what keeps a roller coaster on its track? Why don't we fall out of the car when we're upside down in a loop?

The mechanical engineers who design these rides make sure that they're safe. In the case of the roller coasters and other thrill rides, the key to how they work is *centrifugal force*. This force pushes on the outside when something is making a circular movement. If you swing a bucket full of water around, this force makes the water stay in the bucket even when it's upside down. Along with the safety bar, that same force keeps you in your seat when you're upside down on a coaster loop.

Another scientific concept at work in amusement park rides is gravity, the force used in a free-fall ride. Motors lift riders to the top of the tower. Then gravity takes over, and the excitement begins. With their feet dangling, the riders drop—fast! The ride uses brakes to make gentle stops at several stages. If the brakes slammed on suddenly at the very bottom, riders might injure their necks or backs. Gravity is also the force that makes roller coasters thrilling. Once a train reaches the top of the tallest hill, it is released. Gravity causes it to fly down the tracks, and the energy created by that fall carries the train up the next hill (or loop). Then it falls down again, and the energy carries it up the next hill. If the first hill is tall enough and the roller coaster is well designed, the train can continue for an entire mile (1.6 km)!

Amusement park ride designers want to you feel like you're in danger, but the rides are really very safe. Just make sure your safety harness is on!

Draw Conclusions

When you draw conclusions, you make decisions based on what you read. The information is not stated in the story. You have to figure it out from what is provided. You may need to reread the story to decide the answers.

1. Read the text. What can you tell about Jasmine's personality?

    _____

    _____

2. What can you tell about her mother's personality?

    _____

    _____

3. How did Troy get into the house?

    _____

    _____

4. Did Jasmine's mother draw the wrong conclusion? Explain.

    _____

    _____

Critical Thinking

What do you think happened next?

_____

_____

_____

Remember to Lock Up!

"See you later, honey!" Jasmine's mother called to her as she was leaving for work. "Don't forget to lock up when you leave!"

"Okay, Mom," Jasmine responded. "Have a good day!"

Half an hour later, during her commute to work, Jasmine's mom considered calling Jasmine to remind her again about locking the front door when she left for school. A few weeks earlier, Jasmine had forgotten and the door was left unlocked all day until Jasmine's mom returned home from work. Since then, her mother reminded her every morning—sometimes multiple times.

"You need to be more responsible," Jasmine's mother had scolded. "What if our house had been burglarized while we were gone?" Jasmine felt guilty that she had been so forgetful.

"I promise I'll remember next time, Mom," Jasmine said. In fact, she was so worried about forgetting again that this time she wrote a note to herself—on her hand. As Jasmine was leaving the house, she noticed the note and remembered to grab her key and lock up. She was feeling pretty proud of herself—until she got home after soccer practice. Jasmine's mom was standing outside with her arms crossed in front of her and a stern look on her face.

"I can't believe you forgot to lock the door again," Jasmine's mother said angrily.

"But I'm positive that I locked up this morning," Jasmine insisted.

"Well, the door was unlocked when I got home. Seriously, Jasmine, I can't depend on you to remember anything!" her mother was obviously exasperated.

As they walked into the house, Jasmine heard music coming from upstairs and looked at her mother. Just then, they heard a bedroom door open and out walked Jasmine's older brother, Troy, who attended college three hours away.

"I was wondering when you two would finally get home," Troy said, as he came downstairs. "I decided to drive home this weekend and surprise you."

Draw Conclusions

When you draw conclusions, you make decisions based on what you read. The information is not stated in the story. You have to figure it out from what is provided. You may need to reread the story to decide the answers.

1. Read the text. Why do Indians call Gandhi the father of their nation?

   _____

   _____

   _____

2. Why was Gandhi jailed and threatened?

   _____

   _____

   _____

3. What did Albert Einstein mean by his statement at Gandhi's funeral?

   _____

   _____

   _____

Critical Thinking

Why was Mohandas's name changed to Mahatma?

_____

_____

_____

Mohandas Gandhi

The people of India call Mohandas Gandhi the father of their nation. They call him Mahatma (Great Soul). He was one of the great leaders of the 20th century.

In 1915, the people of India were under British rule. Many of the British laws were unfair to the Indians. Mohandas taught the Indian people *satyagraha*, or nonviolent resistance, to create social and political reform. He would use this method for the rest of his life.

In 1919, new laws took away more freedoms in India. When Mohandas—now called Mahatma—began to work against the laws, he captured the attention of everyone in India and much of the world. The people of India decided to work for their country's independence from Great Britain.

There were many important events during Mohandas's struggle for Indian independence. One of the best known is the Salt March of 1930. Britain charged the Indians a tax on salt, and only the British could make the salt. So, Mohandas led a large group of people on a 165-mile (266 km) march to the Arabian Sea. There, they made salt by evaporating seawater.

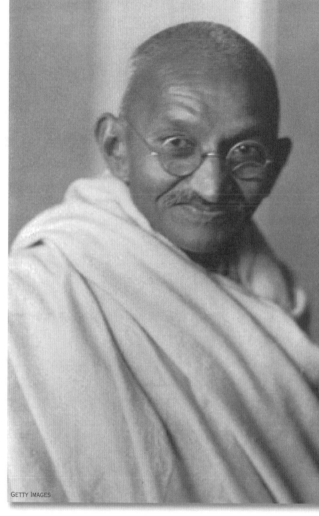

GETTY IMAGES

Although he was sometimes jailed and often threatened, Mohandas continued his peaceful protests. In the year 1947, the world saw the power of his policy of *satyagraha*. After 200 years of British rule, India became a free country.

Unfortunately, Gandhi did not live long after helping India achieve independence. A man shot and killed the peaceful Mahatma in 1948. At Gandhi's funeral, Albert Einstein said, "Generations to come will scarcely believe that such a one as this walked the earth."

Infer

When you infer, you make decisions based on information you read. The information is not given. You have to figure it out from the information provided. You may need to reread the story to decide the answers.

1. Read the text. Can Earth's gravity increase or decrease? Explain.

_____

_____

2. Was Isaac Newton a person who thought for himself? Explain.

_____

_____

3. Jupiter is the largest planet. Explain why Jupiter has more than 60 moons.

_____

_____

Critical Thinking

How does the title relate to the topic of the text?

_____

_____

_____

What Goes Up Must Come Down

Isaac Newton was the first to realize that gravity is the force that makes planets go around the sun and is the same force that makes things fall to Earth. A story about Newton says that he figured out gravity when he saw an apple fall from a tree. He realized that the apple and the moon are similar. Gravity attracts both to Earth.

Gravity is what holds us on the ground and keeps us from floating out into space. It also keeps Earth going around the sun and the moon going around Earth. Without gravity, things would just float around in space.

Isaac Newton

Big Gravity

Watching the planets in the sky, Newton figured out that the planets were pulled toward the sun. The closer the planets were to the sun, the stronger the pull. He also watched the moon. He knew that the moon was moving around Earth. But why did its path curve around instead of shooting away from Earth in a straight line? This seemed to violate Newton's First Law of Motion: objects move in straight lines unless some force makes them change direction.

Newton figured out what must be changing the moon's direction: Earth's gravity. Earth's gravity gives it a constant tug, which keeps it moving around and around in a circle. Think of a ball on a string. If you swing the ball around your head, the tension in the string is like gravity. It keeps the ball moving in a circle. If you were to let go of the string, the ball would fly off at an angle. This is what would happen to the moon if Earth's gravity ceased.

The reason Earth's gravity doesn't make the moon fall down and land on Earth is that the moon has energy from its motion. If something stopped the moon from moving, it would start falling toward Earth. Just as in the ball example, letting the ball slow down too much breaks its "orbit" and makes it fall.

Gravity pulls a diver down toward Earth.

Little Gravity

Everything in the universe exerts a pull of gravity on everything else. The strength of that pull is determined by the object's mass and how far away it is. A big object has a strong pull. A faraway object has a weaker pull. The biggest, closest thing to you is Earth. Since it's big and close, its pull on you is the strongest.

You will never feel it, but you have gravity, too. You have mass, so you have gravity. However, compared to Earth, your gravity is very weak. If you were floating out in space, though, you could have your own tiny "moon" orbiting you. It would have to be really small, though—maybe a pebble!

Infer

When you infer, you make decisions based on information you read. The information is not given. You have to figure it out from the information provided. You may need to reread the story to decide the answers.

1. Read the text. What was the Slinky originally designed to be?

   _____

2. What famous product started out as a means to settle an upset stomach?

   _____

3. How did the 3M scientist who remembered Silver's glue use it?

   _____

   _____

4. Might your parents have played with a Slinky? How do you know?

   _____

   _____

Critical Thinking

What do all of these products have in common?

_____

_____

_____

ACCIDENTAL DISCOVERIES

What do Post-it® notes, Coca-Cola®, and Slinky® toys have in common? All were discovered by accident. That's right—some of the most popular products of all time were stumbled upon accidentally. In most cases, the person who made the discovery was looking for something completely different. They didn't even realize they'd found something useful until years later!

Post-its

One example is the Post-it note—those great little self-stick notepapers. In 1970, chemist Spencer Silver was trying to create a strong glue for his company, 3M. But he wound up with an adhesive that was too weak. It stuck to things, but it could be lifted off easily. He considered it useless. Four years later, another 3M scientist was having a problem keeping his bookmark in his church hymnal while singing in the choir. Then he remembered Silver's glue. Today, Post-it notes are one of the top-selling office products.

Coca-Cola

In 1886 at a drugstore in Atlanta, Georgia, pharmacist John Pemberton mixed carbonated water with a syrup he'd invented. He sold it as a health tonic for five cents per glass. He also gave it to people who felt nauseous, and it calmed their stomachs. After eight years, the drink became popular enough to be sold in bottles. The drugstore's bookkeeper, Frank Robinson, came up with the product's name, and created the cursive-letter logo that's still used today. Now, Coca-Cola is one of the best-known brand names in the world. The company sells more than 1.3 billion drinks every day in 200 countries.

Slinky

Have you ever seen a Slinky "walk" down a flight of stairs? In 1945, inventor Richard James was trying to build a spring for the navy that would keep ship instruments from vibrating. One day, his experiment "walked" off a shelf and down onto the ship's deck! He knew that this would be fun for children to play with. The Slinky remains one of the best-selling toys of all time!

Summarize

A summary sentence tells what a paragraph is about. It may be at the start or the end of a paragraph. If there is no summary sentence, think how you could state the main idea in one sentence.

1. Read the text. Write a summary sentence for each paragraph.

Paragraph 1: _____

_____

Paragraph 2: _____

_____

Paragraph 3: _____

_____

Paragraph 4: _____

_____

Paragraph 5: _____

_____

Critical Thinking

How do summary sentences help you to understand text?

_____

_____

_____

Timing Races

Athletes run races to see who will win. The winners can earn money. They get even more if they break a world record!

Long ago, races were timed using manual stopwatches. But they could only measure down to 0.50 (one-half) of a second. At the 1932 Olympics, automatic stopwatches made their debut. Back then, they could only measure down to 0.10 (one-tenth) of a second. Still, that was a big improvement over the half-second (0.50) of manual stopwatches.

A manual stopwatch

In 1932, the winner of the men's 100-meter race finished in 10.30 seconds. The athlete who finished in third place ran in 10.40 seconds. One-tenth of a second is significant in such a fast race!

Now, digital timers can measure down to 0.001 (one-thousandth) of a second. In addition, a starter gun sets off a digital timer, which is much more exact. The starting blocks have speakers. Runners hear the starter gun through the speakers. They all hear it at the same time. Runners take off when they hear this sound.

A digital timer

The finish line at the 2004 Olympics had a laser beam across it. Runners "broke" the beam as they crossed the line, stopping the timer. This is the most accurate way to time races.

Summarize

A summary sentence tells what a paragraph is about. It may be at the start or the end of a paragraph. If there is no summary sentence, think how you could state the main idea in one sentence.

1. Read the text. Write a summary sentence for the text under the first heading.

    _____

2. Write a summary sentence for the text under the second heading.

    _____

3. Write a summary sentence for the information under the third heading.

    _____

4. Write a short paragraph that summarizes the whole text.

    _____

    _____

    _____

    _____

    _____

Critical Thinking

How does writing a summary of a text help you concentrate on its main idea?

_____

_____

_____

The Iroquois

Life in a Longhouse

The Iroquois people lived in villages of longhouses. These were large wood-frame buildings covered with sheets of elm bark. Iroquois longhouses were up to 100 feet (30.5 m) long or more. Each one housed an entire clan (as many as 60 people). Each had two doors and no windows, with one door located at each end. Inside the longhouses, platforms lined the walls. They were used for sleeping and for storage. The door of each longhouse had a carving or painting of the clan that lived within. This was important because all people of the same clan were related—a large, extended family. Clans were based on an animal ancestor such as a beaver, a hawk, a porcupine, or a turtle.

Food

The Iroquois ate a varied diet because the people farmed, hunted, and fished. The majority of their food came from farming. Iroquois women and children did most of the farming and gathering. They planted crops of corn, beans, and squash. They searched out and harvested wild berries and chestnuts. The food was carefully stored for use during the winter.

Iroquois men did most of the hunting, using bows and arrows to kill deer, elk, and wild turkey. Wherever an Iroquois village was near a river, fishing was also a main food source. Typical Iroquois dishes included cornbread, soups, and stews.

Wampum

Since the Iroquois had no writing system, they relied on the spoken word to pass down their history, rituals, and traditions. In order to help them remember things, the Iroquois created wampum out of white and purple shell beads (made from crab shells). Belts had wampum bead designs that represented significant events. These belts could be used as a kind of currency, but they were more culturally important as an art form and historical record. Why? Most Iroquois traded for what they needed, so money was of little value.

Paraphrase

When you paraphrase, you restate the information in a text in your own words.

1. Read the text. Beginning under the first heading, write one sentence to paraphrase (sum up) each paragraph.

   Paragraph 1: _____

   _____

   Paragraph 2: _____

   _____

   Paragraph 3: _____

   _____

   Paragraph 4: _____

   _____

   Paragraph 5: _____

   _____

Critical Thinking

How did summing up the text in your own words help you to understand what you read?

_____

_____

_____

AFRICAN HISTORY

As the second-largest continent, Africa is bigger than the entire United States and Europe combined. Africa lies south of Europe and southwest of the Middle East.

Long ago, trading goods made the African cultures grow. When empires gained control of trade routes, their power increased. When they lost control of the routes, they lost their power and wealth.

The Kush and the Kingdom of Aksum

The Kush had one of the first civilizations in Africa in what is now the country of Sudan. The people made tools and weapons of iron. Egyptian trade routes passed through the Kush kingdom. The merchants carried ivory, ebony, and animal furs on these routes. Since the Kush owned the roadways, they charged fees to use them. As a result, the Kush became rich.

The Kush carrying ivory tusks

The kingdom of Aksum rose to power in the first century A.D. The Aksum people traded crops, gold, and ivory along the Red Sea's coast. Merchants going to the East passed through Aksum's port city on the Red Sea. This brought the Aksum rulers great wealth and gave them a connection to India, Egypt, and the Roman Empire. Around A.D. 700, Arabs took control of all these trade routes, and the Aksum lost their power.

The Empire of Ghana

The prophet Muhammad began the religion of Islam around A.D. 600. His followers are called Muslims. In the 700s, Muslim traders started to trade gold. They traveled from North Africa to West Africa by moving through the Empire of Ghana.

West Africans in the Empire of Ghana needed a way to keep their food from spoiling. Salt preserved food and made it safe to eat, but West Africans had no way to make their own salt. They did have gold mines, so they traded gold to the Muslims in exchange for salt. Most of the world's gold came from West Africa.

West Africans traded gold for salt.

Ghana owned the major trade routes in northwest Africa. At one point, the Muslims tried to force the people of Ghana to change religions. This led to fighting, which weakened the empire. Then North Africans attacked Ghana and seized the trade routes. By 1203, the Empire of Ghana had been overthrown.

Paraphrase

When you paraphrase, you restate the information in a text in your own words.

1. Read the story. Write five sentences that paraphrase (sum up) the whole story.

_____

_____

_____

_____

_____

_____

_____

_____

_____

_____

Critical Thinking

How does paraphrasing fiction differ from paraphrasing nonfiction?

_____

_____

_____

AZURE MIST SAVES THE DAY

Azure Mist strapped on her tool belt and hopped into the Mist Mobile. Soon, she was zipping along toward Panzer Plaza where a kitten was in danger. As she turned the corner into the Plaza parking lot, she slammed on the brakes. A three-story-tall robotic panther was blocking her path!

"Meeoow!" came a tiny, terrified cry from inside the robot's mouth. Trapped behind enormous silver teeth was a cute, fluffy kitten.

By now, military personnel were setting up rockets to fire at the menacing robot. Azure glanced around her at the various people in the crowd, including a plumber, a teacher, a store clerk, a hairdresser, and an animal catcher.

Azure felt a tingling in the back of her brain. Most superheroes had super strength, the ability to fly, or other extraordinary abilities that allowed them to perform good deeds. However, some relied on specially built gadgets to do their work. Azure Mist was mostly one of these "gadgeteers," although she did have a unique ability that set her apart: she could understand what another being was thinking.

"Wait!" Azure cried. Engaging her hover-boots, she smoothly rose up and spoke directly to the robot. It opened its mouth and allowed Azure to gently pluck out the kitten. The crowd gasped.

"It is all right!" Azure stated in a loud voice after she glided slowly back to the ground. "The robot is programmed to protect cats! It saw the animal catcher and went into action!"

"How did you convince it to let the kitten go?" asked a woman.

"I told it I would adopt her. Now, I will take the robot where it can do the most good. I will use my Mist Mobile to transport it to an animal preserve where it can protect endangered big cats!"

The crowd cheered. Azure Mist had saved the day!

Table of Contents

A table of contents appears at the start of a nonfiction book. It tells the chapters that are in the book. By scanning the table of contents, you can tell if the book might answer a question you have.

1. Scan the table of contents. How many chapters are there in this book? (The index is not a chapter.)

   _____

2. Read the table of contents. Approximately how many pages are in this book? How do you know?

   _____

   _____

3. On what page would you likely find the definition of a Greek city-state? _____

4. In which chapter would you read about pharaohs?

   _____

5. Write the name of the chapter about the kingdoms of Africa.

   _____

Critical Thinking

If you were writing a report on the life of Chandra Gupta I, a famous Indian ruler, would this book provide you with all the information you need? Explain.

_____

_____

_____

World Cultures Through Time

Table of Contents

Table of Contents

A table of contents appears at the start of a nonfiction book. It tells the chapters that are in the book. By scanning the table of contents, you can tell if the book might answer a question you have.

1. Scan the table of contents. What is the name of the chapter that begins on page 29?

   _____

2. Read the table of contents. How many chapters are in this book? (The glossary and index are not chapters.)

   _____

3. On what page would you read about Ashoka? _____

4. About how many pages are in this book? How do you know?

   _____

   _____

Critical Thinking

What information would you expect to find in the chapter titled "Independence"?

_____

_____

_____

India

Table of Contents

Index

An index is always on the last pages of a nonfiction book. It is a list of important topics that are covered in the book. Specific words and ideas are given their own listings. If you want to see if a word is mentioned in a book, use the index.

1. Scan the index. How are the entries listed—in the order in which they appear in the book or alphabetically? How do you know?

   _____

   _____

2. On what page(s) would you find information about blizzards? _____

3. If you turned to page 26, what would you read about? _____

4. If you wanted to learn about thunderstorms, what is the first page to which you would turn?

   _____

5. Does this book discuss tsunamis? How can you tell?

   _____

   _____

Critical Thinking

How does a book's index differ from its table of contents?

_____

_____

_____

Index

Index

An index is always on the last pages of a nonfiction book. It is a list of important topics that are covered in the book. Specific words and ideas are given their own listings. If you want to see if a word is mentioned in a book, use the index.

1. Read the index. On what pages would you find information about the industrialist John D. Rockefeller?

    _____

2. If you turned to page 14, whom would you read about?

    _____

3. If you wanted to learn about labor unions, to which page would you turn?

    _____

4. Is the Gospel of Wealth discussed in this book? How do you know?

    _____

    _____

    _____

Critical Thinking

Why isn't there an index in the back of a fiction book?

_____

_____

_____

INDUSTRIAL GIANTS

Index

Glossary

A glossary is like a very short dictionary placed in the back of a nonfiction book. The glossary lists the definitions of important words used in the book. If you are reading and don't understand a word, turn to the glossary.

1. Scan the glossary on the next page. You will see some words you may not know. List two below.

   _____   _____

2. Read the text. Write the definition for one of the words you listed above.

   _____

   _____

3. Describe the term *acid rain* in your own words.

   _____

   _____

4. What word means "living in water"?

   _____

5. Name an animal that is extinct.

   _____

Critical Thinking

How does a glossary differ from an index?

_____

_____

_____

Inside Ecosystems

Glossary

acid rain—any precipitation that contains sulfuric and nitric acid caused by chemicals released from burning fossil fuels

altitude (AL-tih-tood)—how far something is above sea level

aquatic (uh-KWOT-ik)—living or growing in water

biome (BYE-ohm)—a large area that shares the same general climate of temperature and rainfall

climate (KLYE-mit)—the usual weather in a place

community (kuh-MYOO-nuh-tee)—the plants and animals living together in a habitat

consumer (kuhn-SOO-mur)—an animal that eats

decomposer (dee-kuhm-POZ-er)—an earthworm, bacterium, or fungus that breaks down dead plants and animals

ecosystem (EE-koh-sis-tuhm)—the interaction between a community of plants and animals living in a natural environment

endangered (en-DAYN-jurd)—a plant or animal with such few numbers that it may become extinct

extinct (ek-STINGKT)—a plant or animal that has completely died out; there will never be any more like it

fertilizer (FUR-tuh-lye-zur)—any substance put on fields or lawns to make crops or grass grow better

global warming—the rising surface temperature of Earth caused by increasing amounts of carbon dioxide and other gases in the atmosphere

habitat (HAB-uh-tat)—the natural home of an animal or a plant

permafrost (PUR-muh-frost)—a soil layer below the ground that stays frozen for two or more years in an area where the average air temperature remains below 18°F

photosynthesis (foh-toh-SIN-thuh-siss)—a chemical process by which green plants make their own food

taiga (TIE-guh)—pine forests that border the tundra; largest land biome on Earth

Glossary

A glossary is like a very short dictionary placed in the back of a nonfiction book. The glossary lists the definitions of important words used in the book. If you are reading and don't understand a word, turn to the glossary.

1. Scan the glossary on the next page. You will see some words you may not know. List two below.

    _____   _____

2. Read the text. Write the definition for one of the words you listed above.

    _____

    _____

3. What is the instrument that is used to measure the amount of water in the air?

    _____

4. Use the word *climate* in a sentence.

    _____

    _____

Critical Thinking

When would you use a glossary?

_____

_____

_____

Earth's Atmosphere

Glossary

air pressure—the density, or weight, of air pushing down on Earth's surface

atmosphere (AT-mus-feer)—a layer of air that covers the entire Earth and controls our temperature

Celsius (SEL-see-uhss) **scale**—a measurement of temperature using a scale on which water boils at 100 degrees and freezes at 0 degrees; originally called centigrade scale

centigrade (SEN-tuh-grade) **scale**—Celsius' original name for his temperature scale which was divided into 100 parts; now called the Celsius scale

climate (KLYE-mit)—the usual weather in a place

climatology (klye-muh-TAWL-uh-jee)—the study of the general weather patterns in a given area over a long period of time

Fahrenheit (FAIR-uhn-hite) **scale**—a measurement of temperature using a scale on which fresh water boils at 212 degrees and freezes at 32 degrees

hygrometer (hy-GROM-uh-tur)—an instrument for measuring the amount of water in the air (humidity)

lightning—a flash of high-voltage electricity that moves from one charged cloud to another or from a charged cloud to the ground

mercury (MUR-cure-ree)—a poisonous silver liquid metal used in thermometers and barometers

meteorology (mee-tee-uh-ROL-uh-jee)—the study of Earth's atmosphere, climates, and weather

radar—a device used to find solid objects by reflecting radio waves off them and by receiving the reflected waves; originally an acronym for Radio Detecting and Ranging

temperature—a degree of heat or cold as measured by a thermometer

thermometer—an instrument that measures temperature

troposphere (TROH-puhs-feer)—the part of the atmosphere closest to Earth's surface where all weather occurs

weather satellite (SAT-uh-lite)—a spacecraft sent into orbit miles above Earth that continuously monitors and photographs conditions in the atmosphere

Answer Key

Predict, p. 8

1. Answers will vary. Sample: I think this text will be about playing soccer.
2. Answers will vary. Sample: From the title and photo, it could be a story or nonfiction. However, glancing at the text, I see the title of a book in italics, which makes me think it is nonfiction.
3. Answers will vary. Sample: Yes, the author presents both sides of the story by telling both the benefits and drawbacks of competitive sports for children.
4. Answers will vary. Sample: I predict that Aidan Wolfe will continue to play soccer because it means so much to him.

Critical Thinking answers will vary. Sample: My prediction for #1 was wrong because the text was about playing all sorts of sports. I was right about questions 2 and 3.

Predict, p. 10

1. Answers will vary. Sample: On my first day at a new school, I wanted my teacher to know I was excited to learn.
2. Answers will vary. Sample: I think the story will be about a person who has a crush on someone.
3. Answers will vary. Sample: I don't think that Arturo or Charlene have any idea how the other person feels about him or her because both of them are very nervous about seeing each other.

Critical Thinking answers will vary. Sample: This story is humorous because both characters are nervous, and they don't have any reason to be because the other person likes them just as much.

Prior Knowledge, p. 12

1. Answers will vary. Sample: Birds have feathers; They are warm blooded; They lay eggs.
2. Answers will vary. Sample: I like camping because I think it's fun to sleep outside.
3. Answers will vary. Sample: Yes, it sounds like the author wants to take up bird watching as a new hobby.

Critical Thinking answers will vary. Sample: I didn't want to try snorkeling because I was scared. Now I enjoy it, and it's one of my favorite activities.

Prior Knowledge, p. 14

1. Answers will vary. Sample: They live in Africa on the savannah; they live in prides.
2. Answers will vary. Sample: I think that Gamba will be a lion.
3. Answers will vary. Sample: The intruder that alarms Gamba is some sort of vehicle, perhaps a bush jeep or a safari vehicle. I know because of the burning oil smell, which is probably exhaust fumes.

Critical Thinking answers will vary. Sample: No, I had to use prior knowledge because the author wanted me to view the intruder through Gamba's eyes.

Set a Purpose, p. 16

1. Answers will vary. Sample: What is the Heimlich maneuver?
2. Answers will vary. Accept any two facts about the Heimlich maneuver.
3. Answers will vary. Sample: I wish the passage told how to determine that the choking is serious enough to use the Heimlich maneuver.

Critical Thinking answers will vary. Sample: Yes, the text explains that the Heimlich maneuver is a technique to expel an object from a person's windpipe.

Set a Purpose, p. 18

1. Answers will vary. Sample: The title is unusual because the two words are opposites—something that is mundane is not mysterious.
2. Answers will vary. Sample: This story will be about someone getting a haircut.
3. Answers will vary. Sample: Jonathan wanted a new look, and he had somewhere important to go with a man in a suit.
4. Answers will vary. Sample: Yes, I understood the title better after I'd read the story because getting a haircut is mundane, but the way it is presented made me wonder what is going on and why Jonathan needs his hair cut so short.

Critical Thinking answers will vary. Sample: Yes, the text left me wondering why Jonathan needed a short haircut, who the man in dark clothes is, and where they are going to go.

Answer Key (cont.)

Ask Questions, p. 20

1. Answers will vary. Sample: Where is the Great Pacific Garbage Patch?
2. Answers will vary. Sample: How did all of this trash get into the water?
3. Answers will vary. Sample: It is made from waste gathered from storm drains; It may be as big as the state of Texas.

Critical Thinking answers will vary. Sample: Yes, the text said that the trash got into the water from liter being washed down storm drains.

Ask Questions, p. 22

1. Answers will vary. Sample: Why is John Barry called the Father of the American Navy?
2. Answers will vary. Sample: Did John Barry invent the American Navy?
3. Answers will vary. Sample: Barry was made the first captain of the U.S. Navy; He captured the *HMS Edward*.
4. Answers will vary. Sample: It is important to learn about John Barry because he helped to establish the U.S. Navy. Without a navy, the history of the United States might be very different.

Critical Thinking answers will vary. Sample: No, but I can look it up online, in an encyclopedia, or in a library book.

Make Connections, p. 24

1. Answers will vary. Sample: I learned how to play the piano.
2. Answers will vary. Sample: I had to try over and over and practice a lot.
3. Answers will vary. Sample: The ending is a surprise because the beginning makes it sound like William and Marcus are professional skiers, not beginners.
4. Answers will vary. Sample: My understanding of William changed because I started out thinking that he was an Olympic skier in a major competition but he is a kid just learning how to ski.

Critical Thinking answers will vary. Sample: Making connections helped me to understand the boys' mindset because I sometimes fantasize that I'm in the X Games when I am doing tricks on my skateboard.

Make Connections, p. 26

1. Answers will vary. Sample: I went skiing with my aunt and uncle so I know that a person wears skis and uses poles.
2. Answers will vary. Sample: I am most familiar with NASCAR. I enjoy the sport because it's fun to see cars driving at such high speeds.
3. Answers will vary. Sample: Yes, it be would be an exciting competition because the skiers are racing down a course with lots of twists and turns.

Critical Thinking answers will vary. Sample: Answering the questions before I read this text helped me to understand ski cross because it made me think about what I already know about the other sports mentioned in the text.

Context Clues, p. 28

1. Answers will vary. Sample: The word *ominous* means "threatening, menacing, dangerous." I know because the smoke terrifies the crew.
2. Answers will vary. Sample: The word *transfixed* means "frozen in place; unable to move." I know because the text says that the crew stood at the ship's rails and watched a volcano erupt right in front of them. If I saw that, I wouldn't be able to move.
3. Answers will vary. Sample: The word *barren* means "bare." I know because the text says that the black rock was without animals or plants on it.

Critical Thinking answers will vary. Sample: Using context clues lets me read more difficult texts because I can use the sentences and words around the words I don't understand to figure out what they mean.

Use Context Clues, p. 30

1. Answers will vary. Sample: The word *version* means "form, kind, or type". I know because I can substitute any of those words for version, and the sentence still makes sense.
2. Answers will vary. Sample: The word *consumed* means "ate." I know because it says they are plant eaters and also they consumed plants.
3. Answers will vary. Sample: The word *dissipate* means "to scatter or disperse." I know because the elephant's big ears are trying to get rid of body heat.

Critical Thinking answers will vary. Sample: Using context clues helped me to understand the function of an elephants ear—to dissipate heat.

Answer Key *(cont.)*

Visualize, p. 32

1. Pictures will vary but should show a person waking up, moving across the bedroom to the alarm clock on the dresser, or trying to hit the clock to turn it off.
2. Pictures will vary but should show a person pressing the alarm clock button with his or her nose, a person pressing the alarm clock button with his or her elbow, a person sitting on the alarm clock, a person trying to use a toe to poke the button of the clock on the floor.
3. Pictures will vary but should show a person running down the hall, pushing on the alarm button, or falling back into bed.

Critical Thinking answers will vary. Sample: Picturing what was in the text let me "see" how funny this story was as I pictured the poor kid trying to turn off the alarm clock.

Visualize, p. 34

1. Pictures will vary but should show a brave boy, a horse throwing the king off its back, or the king sending the horse away.
2. Pictures will vary but should show Alexander speaking with his father, Alexander leading the horse, or Alexander getting into the saddle.
3. Pictures will vary but should show Alexander riding the horse as the crowd cheers him, Alexander astride the horse speaking to his father, or Alexander riding the horse into battle.

Critical Thinking answers will vary. Sample: It was like making a movie in my mind, so I saw the story unfold as it happened.

Conflict and Resolution, p. 36

1. Kenny is a student, and Mrs. Melba is his teacher.
2. Answers will vary. Sample: A muse is someone who provides artists with their inspiration, based of the nine daughters of Zeus and Mnemosyne.
3. Answers will vary. Sample: Kenny's conflict is that he has an assignment to write a story, but he can't think of a story line.
4. Answers will vary. Sample: The resolution is that Kenny realizes that he can write about his dream and create his own ending.

Critical Thinking answers will vary. Sample: Kenny's imagination provided him with inspiration for a story while he was dreaming.

Conflict and Resolution, p. 38

1. Answers will vary. Sample: Juanita is a member of a band called The Undead Chipmunks. She's annoyed because they've had three drummers quit the band, and now the new drummer is late to practice.
2. Answers will vary. Sample: The conflict is that they have a paying gig to prepare for and they don't have a drummer.
3. Answers will vary. Sample: The resolution is that the drummer, a squirrel, arrives and is a great musician.

Critical Thinking answers will vary. Sample: I would not like a story that has the problem solved quickly because it wouldn't build suspense.

Characters, p. 40

1. Answers will vary. Sample: An eagle will be a character in the story.
2. Answers will vary. Sample:
   Eagle's Personality: She is too trusting or gullible, and she is desperate for a mate.
   Kite's Personality: He is devious and dishonest. He tricks the Eagle into marrying him with false promises.
3. Answers will vary. Sample: The Kite is more to blame because he told lies to get the Eagle to marry him.

Critical Thinking answers will vary. Sample: The moral is to not believe outrageous promises, no matter how much you want them to be true.

Characters, p. 42

1. Answers will vary. Sample: The story will be about a new chess player.
2. Answers will vary. Sample: Sheila is very organized and efficient. She doesn't tolerate any nonsense and isn't afraid of anyone, even a monster.
3. Answers will vary. Sample: The other members of the Chess Club feel that Sheila is bossy, but they respect her.
4. Answers will vary. Sample: My friend is like Sheila. She went on a trip with me and told me what to do every minute.

Critical Thinking answers will vary. Sample: Sheila steals the show because she reacts in an unexpected way to Bruno. Her behavior is so bold that it's outrageous.

Answer Key (cont.)

Literary Devices, p. 44

1. Answers will vary. Sample: "hung like chimpanzees from his tie"
2. Answers will vary. Sample: "clung tighter than a barnacle to the hull of a fishing trawler"
3. Answers will vary. Sample: You can infer that the writer is an adult recalling his life with his father, who is now deceased.

Critical Thinking answers will vary. Sample: Literary devices make reading more interesting because they create interesting mental images.

Literary Devices, p. 46

1. Answers will vary. Sample: "dark wall of clouds marched toward us like a solemn, deadly army"
2. Answers will vary. Sample: "sandblasting our faces"
3. Answers will vary. Sample: "the red sunset bled through the storm clouds"

Critical Thinking answers will vary. Accept any verb as long as there is an explanation for why that verb was selected.

Literary Themes, p. 48

1. Answers will vary. Sample: The theme is that having a friend is more important than being part of the popular crowd. I know because the author is horrified that she denied her friend and rushes to repair the relationship.
2. Answers will vary. Sample: The author wants the reader to realize that it is never a good idea to speak against a good friend no matter what the circumstances are.
3. Answers will vary. Sample: At the start, the narrator is delighted that the popular girls want to include her, but later she dislikes them because they tricked her.

Critical Thinking answers will vary. I read a story about a man who is in love with a woman who does not love him back.

Literary Themes, p. 50

1. Answers will vary. Sample: The theme is humor. I know because the point of the whole story is to make the reader laugh.
2. Answers will vary. Sample: The author wrote this story to entertain the reader. The author tells about a time when he messes up his single line in a school play to make the reader laugh.
3. Answers will vary. Sample: No, I think that he had a bad enough experience being in this play that he'll never want to do it again.

Critical Thinking answers will vary. Sample: The author uses humor because he or she wants to make the reader laugh and wants the story to be interesting.

Title and Headings, p. 52

1. Answers will vary. Sample: I think the text will be about the U.S. Census.
2. The text has three headings.
3. Counting People: Every 10 years, all the people living in the United States get counted in a census; Collecting the Census: Most people get their census forms in the mail, fill them out, and mail them back. Census workers must visit the people who do not do so; Using the Data: Governments, schools, and rescue workers are just a few of the organizations that need to use the census data.

Critical Thinking answers will vary. Sample: The headings make it easier to find specific information quickly. You can scan it to find what you need to know.

Title and Headings, p. 54

1. Answers will vary. Sample: The text will be about Leonardo da Vinci.
2. The text has three headings.
3. Answers will vary. Sample: I can infer that da Vinci was talented in art, engineering, and science.
4. Answers will vary. Sample: Yes, my inference was correct. Leonardo da Vinci was famous as an artist, an engineer, and a scientist.

Critical Thinking answers will vary. Sample: The writer used headings to divide this text into sections to help the reader to focus on each of da Vinci's three major talents.

Answer Key *(cont.)*

Typeface and Captions, p. 56

1. I see normal typeface and italics.
2. Answers will vary. Sample: Most of the words are in normal typeface, and two vocabulary words are in italics.
3. Answers will vary. Sample: These definitions are included because these words are important to understanding the text.
4. Answers will vary. Sample: It shows me what Washington's mansion, Mount Vernon, looked like.
5. Answers will vary. Sample: The new information in the caption is that Blue Skin was one of Washington's favorite horses.

Critical Thinking answers will vary. Sample: The word *plantation* could have been defined. I chose this word because it is important to understanding where Washington lived.

Typeface and Captions, p. 58

1. I see normal, boldface, and italics typeface in this text.
2. Answers will vary. Sample: Most of the text appears in normal typeface. The heading is in boldface, and the key vocabulary terms are in italics.
3. Answers will vary. Sample: The writer wanted to make the heading stand out with boldface. The writer also wanted to identify the key vocabulary terms with italics.
4. Answers will vary. Sample: The captions helped me to understand how complex a food web is.

Critical Thinking answers will vary. Sample: Plankton are at the start of the food web and polar bears are at the top because they are the largest predator. There are billions of plankton and only a few polar bears because energy is lost at each level of the "pyramid."

Graphics, p. 60

1. 8:00 A.M.
2. Tuesday, Thursday
3. You will need to bring your own glove.
4. Answers will vary. Sample: The information missing is the time(s) that you can get your dog washed. You can call Lisa at the number on the newsletter.

Critical Thinking answers will vary. Sample: I used a message board at school to find out when the chess club meets.

Graphics, p. 62

1. Answers will vary. Sample: I think microbes are germs that cause diseases.
2. Answers will vary. Sample: bacteria, fungi, protozoa
3. The protozoa entamoeba is shown in the bottom picture.
4. Answers will vary. Sample: The word *resistance* means "the ability to fight off germs." I know because the text gives the definition of this word immediately after using it.

Critical Thinking answers will vary. Sample: The microbes' photos were taken under a microscope so that they have been magnified.

Topic Sentences, p. 64

1. The Vikings were a group of people whose sailors explored the North Atlantic Ocean from A.D. 700 to 1100.
2. Over the years, the Vikings became expert ship builders.
3. The Vikings believed that the ships would endow these people with a safe journey to the land of the dead.

Critical Thinking answers will vary. Sample: The topic sentences give the main ideas about Vikings so I could use them to write a summary of the text.

Topic Sentences, p. 66

1. Florida's nickname is the Sunshine State.
2. Like many southern states, Florida's climate is good for growing food.
3. Florida's weather isn't always pleasant.

Critical Thinking answers will vary. Sample: The next time I read a nonfiction text, I will look for topic sentences to guide me through the text.

Main Idea, p. 68

1. The main character is Marla.
2. Answers will vary. Sample: Marla works at a sea park, and her job is to train dolphins.
3. Answers will vary. Sample: The main idea is that Marla is having her first independent training session with the porpoises.

Critical Thinking answers will vary. Sample: Finding the main idea of fiction differs because the story will not clearly state a main idea in a sentence.

Main Idea, p. 70

1. Answers will vary. Sample: The author wrote this text to encourage kids to try to make simple recipes and snacks for themselves.
2. Answers will vary. Sample: The focus changes to a recipe for an omelet.
3. Answers will vary. Sample: The main idea is that kids can make simple recipes and snacks by themselves, starting with making an omelet.

Critical Thinking answers will vary. Sample: If you don't do everything in the order it says, you could end up with an inedible mess.

Details, p. 72

1. Ricky Sharpton, Jocelyn Ricci
2. Answers will vary. Sample: The main idea is that the Ellis Junior High Key Club is holding a blood drive to help a student and other members of the community who need blood.
3. Answers will vary. Sample:
   What: blood drive
   When: January 18 from 10 A.M.–2 P.M.
   Where: Ellis Junior High School multipurpose room
   Who: people aged 16 and up in good health
   Why: to help Ricky Sharpton and other sick people in the community

Critical Thinking answers will vary. Sample: The details in fiction are not necessarily true. The details in nonfiction text are facts.

Details, p. 74

1. The book's title is *Uncle Tom's Cabin*.
2.–3. Answers will vary. Sample:

Main Idea: Harriet Beecher Stowe wrote *Uncle Tom's Cabin*, a popular book. It helped the antislavery cause in the North but caused outrage in the South.
Detail: The book tells about the lives of two slave families.
Detail: Readers became involved in the story and cared about the slaves.
Detail: The book broke all sales records.
Detail: The book made Southerners so furious that it was illegal to have it in some places.

Critical Thinking answers will vary. Sample: I looked for which details best supported the main idea and included those.

Main Idea and Details, p. 76

1. Main Idea: Domesticated rats make great pets.
2. Answers will vary. Sample: Details: Rats are social and intelligent; Rats bond with their families and enjoy cuddling with humans; Rats rarely bite, learn their names, and can learn how to do tricks; Responsible owners should keep rats in pairs.

Critical Thinking answers will vary. Sample: I looked for facts that best supported the main idea.

Main Idea and Details, p. 78

1. Answers will vary. Sample: Main Idea: Deciduous trees have a hormone that sends a message to their leaves to drop in the autumn.
2. Answers will vary. Sample: Details: When the days get shorter and colder, the hormone is triggered; A thin, bumpy line of cells forms where each leaf stem meets its branch; This line of cells cuts the leaf off from the tree; The tree must get rid of its old leaves before they freeze and die.

Critical Thinking answers will vary. Sample: I looked for which details best supported the main idea and included those.

Main Idea and Details, p. 80

1. The main character is Jason.
2. Answers will vary. Sample: He was close to Eddie before he moved away and now he wonders if it will be awkward to see him again.
3. Answers will vary. Sample: Eddie gives Jason a bear hug and they run off to play a video game together.
4. Answers will vary. Sample: The main idea is that people who have been apart for a while can reconnect as if they had not parted at all.

Critical Thinking answers will vary. Sample: I think it is easier to find the main idea and details in nonfiction because it is usually stated clearly in one or two sentences.

Answer Key *(cont.)*

Chronological Order, p. 82

1.

1978	NASA chose Sally to train as an astronaut.
1982	Sally was a crewmember on a space shuttle flight and the first U.S. woman in space.
1984	Sally flew on the *Challenger* shuttle, too.
1986	The *Challenger* blew up.
1987	Sally left NASA to work at Stanford University.

Critical Thinking answers will vary. Sample: Authors write events in chronological order because it makes the most sense to readers.

Chronological Order, p. 84

1. 1, 4, 5, 3, 2
2. 20 years old
3. 81 years old

Critical Thinking answers will vary. Sample: Abigail's determination to learn changed the course of her life because it enabled her to discuss political decisions with her husband when he became president.

Logical Order, p. 86

1. 3, 6, 4, 2, 1, 5
2. Answers will vary. Sample: My mother promised me a puppy from the shelter as soon as the yard was cleaned up. I was so happy that I helped finish the yard.
3. Answers will vary. Sample: The hardest part was worrying that all the puppies would be gone by the time I got to the shelter.

Critical Thinking answers will vary. Sample: I think the hardest part for Randy will be earning enough money to buy all the parts that are needed to fix up the old car.

Logical Order, p. 88

1. Answers will vary. Sample: No, I can't use soil straight out of my backyard because the dirt has to contain humus, leaf mold, and potting soil.
2. Answers will vary. Sample: Yes, the steps need to be done in the order given. You are trying to create a miniature, closed ecosystem, which is not as easy as it might appear.
3. Answers will vary. Sample: The plants might die if you don't put the terrarium where it will get the right amount of light.

Critical Thinking answers will vary. Sample: It appears that the most difficult part of making a terrarium is getting the moisture level right.

Fact and Opinion, p. 90

1. Answers will vary. Sample: The writer's grandfather lived minutes away from an amusement park.
2. Answers will vary. Sample: I bet you can't wait to ride the roller coasters!
3. O, F, O, F, F

Critical Thinking answers will vary. Sample: The author makes her grandfather sound like an interesting man, and maybe he would teach me to water ski!

Fact and Opinion, p. 92

1. F, O, F, F, O
2. Answers will vary. Sample: The air is holding 10 percent of all the water vapor it can hold. The air would feel dry at 10 percent humidity.

Critical Thinking answers will vary. Sample: A weather forecast should consist of facts and opinions. The facts are the statistics for the day, such as the high and low temperatures. Opinions will make it more interesting.

Proposition and Support, p. 94

1. Answers will vary. Sample: The writer's proposition will be that we need to take action to preserve our national parks.
2. Answers will vary. Sample: There are too many cars that cause pollution and run over wildlife; People are careless with fire; Oil and gas that spill from boats' motors pollute water.
3. Answers will vary. Samples: Make sure the public lands cannot be sold to investors; Limit the number of tourists' cars allowed into the parks and forbid motorboats near coastal parks.
4. Answers will vary. Sample: Some of the groups who might protest against the writer's ideas are snowmobilers and oil companies.

Critical Thinking answers will vary. Sample: The writer persuaded me that his or her ideas are good because I think that the national parks are in danger.

Proposition and Support, p. 96

1. Answers will vary. Sample: The writer's proposition will be about how amazing it is to travel to space.
2. The two nations involved in the space race were the United States and the Soviet Union.
3. Answers will vary. Sample: The author is enthusiastic about space exploration. I know because the writer uses positive adjectives to promote the ISS ("wonderful laboratory") and the spacecraft New Horizons ("important data").
4. Answers will vary. Sample: A manned trip to the moon is planned for 2018; There are plans for a long visit to Mars.
5. Answers will vary. Sample: One argument against space exploration is that it costs a lot of money. That money could be used to help the poor.

Critical Thinking answers will vary. Student must state if he or she thinks that exploring space is worth the cost and provide a brief rationale.

Author's Purpose, p. 98

1. Answers will vary. Sample: The author wrote this text to encourage pet owners to spay or neuter their animals.
2. Answers will vary. Sample: The author feels that animal shelters are offering an important service. At the end, the author encourages the reader to donate time or money to an animal shelter.
3. Approximately 4 million shelter animals found homes [The number of animals entering shelters last year (7 million) minus the number euthanized (3 million)].
4. Answers will vary. Sample: The author included this information so that the reader understands that pet overpopulation is a huge problem that costs millions of animals their lives every year.

Critical Thinking answers will vary. Sample: I would most likely read a text like this in in a magazine that was about pets or a newspaper editorial.

Author's Purpose, p. 100

1. Answers will vary. Sample: The author wrote this text to educate readers about sea turtles and the need to protect them.
2. Answers will vary. Sample: The author is against turtle poachers.
3. Answers will vary. Sample: Tourists come to see the sea turtles nest, and this benefits the community by bringing in cash.
4. Answers will vary. Sample: The author hopes the reader will believe that it is important to protect sea turtles.

Critical Thinking answers will vary. Sample: Scientists know where the sea turtles lay their eggs because the females return to nest on the same beach where they hatched. Since all sea turtles follow this pattern, it is well known which beaches have turtle egg nests.

Compare and Contrast, p. 102

1. Your Options: 2-yr or 4-yr, technical or online; large or small; one of a crowd or personal attention; sports teams or not; at home or on campus; in the country; in the suburbs; in a city
2. Answers will vary. Accept any reasonable responses.

Critical Thinking answers will vary. Sample: Choosing a college is important because a person needs to attend the school that best fits his or her needs.

Compare and Contrast, p. 104

1. Answers will vary. Sample: nonrenewable energy: gas, oil, coal (fossil fuels); created from the bodies of dead plants and animals; world has used them for more than 100 years; within about 40 years we will completely run out; create pollution renewable energy: wind, solar, do not cause pollution; we will not run out; do not pollute both: types of energy; create electricity

Critical Thinking answers will vary. Sample: I believe that solar energy is more useful because most people can put solar panels on their roofs but cannot build windmills to capture the wind's energy.

Answer Key *(cont.)*

Cause and Effect, p. 106

1. Answers will vary. Sample: Phil Michaels was always in trouble, getting in fights, or staying out past the team curfew. On the field, he argued with the umpires or attacked pitchers.
2. Answers will vary. Sample: Diego admired that Phil Michaels was a very talented ball player.
3. Answers will vary. Sample: When Diego acted like Phil Michaels, his friends and teachers began to dislike Diego.
4. Answers will vary. Sample: Diego stopped admiring Phil Michaels after the baseball player was extremely rude to him.

Critical Thinking answers will vary. Sample: Most sports heroes who act badly end up getting kicked off their teams.

Cause and Effect, p. 108

1. Gravity causes a roller coaster to follow its track.
2. Centrifugal force (and a safety bar) causes a rider to stay inside an upside-down coaster car.
3. The effect of the brakes on the free-fall ride is to slow it down gradually rather than too suddenly.
4. Releasing a roller coaster train at the top of the highest hill causes it to rush to the bottom of the hill and then up to the top of the next hill.

Critical Thinking answers will vary. Sample: People like amusement rides because they want to be scared and thrilled while staying safe.

Draw Conclusions, p. 110

1. Answers will vary. Sample: Jasmine is obedient and doesn't want to disappoint her mother again.
2. Answers will vary. Sample: Jasmine's mother is a worrier. She is fearful about leaving the house unlocked so she pressures Jasmine to remember to lock the door.
3. Answers will vary. Sample: Troy probably had his own key to the house.
4. Answers will vary. Sample: Yes, Jasmine's mother drew the wrong conclusion that Jasmine had left the door unlocked when her brother had come home unexpectedly.

Critical Thinking answers will vary. Sample: I think that Jasmine's mother will apologize to her for not believing that she remembered to lock the door when she left for school.

Draw Conclusions, p. 112

1. Answers will vary. Sample: Indians call him the father of their nation because he convinced the British to let India be its own nation again.
2. Answers will vary. Sample: Gandhi was jailed and threatened because he was encouraging people to resist the British leadership of India.
3. Answers will vary. Sample: Albert Einstein meant that Gandhi was such an amazing man that he seemed too good to be true.

Critical Thinking answers will vary. Sample: Mohandas's name was changed to Mahatma because he was a "great soul" in persevering against all odds and without violence.

Infer, p. 114

1. Answers will vary. Sample: No, because gravity is based on an object's mass, and Earth's mass remains the same at all times.
2. Answers will vary. Sample: Yes, Isaac Newton was a person who thought for himself. He was the first person able to figure out why gravity exists and exactly how it functions.
3. Answers will vary. Sample: Jupiter has so much mass that its gravity pulls smaller objects toward it and they start to orbit it as moons.

Critical Thinking answers will vary. Sample: The title states a basic fact about gravity, and then the text explains gravity.

Answer Key *(cont.)*

Infer, p. 116
1. The Slinky originally was designed to be a spring for navy ships.
2. Coca-Cola started out as a drink to settle an upset stomach.
3. Answers will vary. Sample: The 3M scientist who remembered Silver's glue used it to create a sticky bookmark for his hymnal.
4. Answers will vary. Sample: Yes, my parents might have played with a Slinky because it has been around for 65 years, and my parents are younger than that.

Critical Thinking answers will vary. Sample: All of these products were originally designed for some other purpose and then later turned into famous, popular products.

Summarize, p. 118
1. Answers will vary. Sample:
   Paragraph 1: Athletes run races to win money and break records.
   Paragraph 2: Long ago, races were timed using manual stopwatches.
   Paragraph 3: One-tenth of a second makes a big difference in a fast race like the 100-meter.
   Paragraph 4: Now digital timers can measure to one-thousandth of a second.
   Paragraph 5: A laser-beam finish line is the most accurate way to time races.

Critical Thinking answers will vary. Sample: Summary sentences help me to understand the text because they make clear what each paragraph is going to talk about.

Summarize, p. 120
1. Answers will vary. Sample: The Iroquois lived in family groups based on clans inside large wood-frame buildings called longhouses.
2. Answers will vary. Sample: The Iroquois ate a varied diet based mostly on farming but also on hunting and fishing.
3. Answers will vary. Sample: The Iroquois made wampum belts using white and purple shell beads to create designs that represented significant events in their history.
4. Answers will vary. Sample: The Iroquois lived in family groups based on clans inside large wood-frame buildings called longhouses. They ate a varied diet based mostly on farming but also on hunting and fishing. The people made wampum belts using white and purple shell beads to create designs that represented significant events in their history.

Critical Thinking answers will vary. Sample: Writing a summary of a text helps me to concentrate on its main idea because I have to decide what to include and what to eliminate.

Paraphrase, p. 122
1. Answers will vary. Sample:
   Paragraph 1: The Kush had one of the first civilizations in Africa and became rich from the fees traders paid to use their roadways.
   Paragraph 2: The kingdom of Aksum was connected to many other nations through a trade system until it fell to the Arabs around A.D. 700.
   Paragraph 3: Islam's followers, called Muslims, were traders that moved through the Empire of Ghana.
   Paragraph 4: West Africans exchanged salt for gold with the Muslims.
   Paragraph 5: When the Muslims tried to force the people of Ghana to change religions, fighting weakened the empire, and by 1203 the North Africans had seized the trade routes.

Critical Thinking answers will vary. Sample: Summing up the text in my own words helped me to understand what I read because I had to think about the main idea and which details were most important.

Answer Key *(cont.)*

Paraphrase, p. 124

1. Answers will vary. Sample: Azure Mist is a superhero who has the ability to know what others are thinking. She rushes to save a kitten from the mouth of a gigantic robotic panther. The military plans to destroy the robot with a rocket, but Azure speaks to the robot. After Azure promises to adopt the kitten, the robot allows her to bring it down to the ground, ending the crisis. She says she will use her Mist Mobile to transport the robot to an animal preserve where it will protect endangered big cats.

Critical Thinking answers will vary. Sample: Paraphrasing fiction is different from paraphrasing nonfiction because you can just tell what happened in the story without trying to remember facts.

Table of Contents, p. 126

1. 15 chapters
2. Answers will vary. Sample: There are at least 146 pages. I know because the index begins on page 146.
3. page 61
4. "Rulers of Ancient Egypt"
5. "African Kingdoms"

Critical Thinking answers will vary. Sample: This book probably wouldn't provide all the information I need because there are only eight pages devoted to all Indian rulers. I'd probably need a book with a whole chapter on Chandra Gupta I.

Table of Contents, p. 128

1. "Moving Into the Modern World"
2. 13 chapters
3. page 16
4. There are about 33 pages in this book. I know because the index begins on page 33, and that is the last part of the book.

Critical Thinking answers will vary. Sample: I would expect to find out when India became an independent nation and about India's form of government as an independent nation.

Index, p. 130

1. The entries are listed alphabetically. Explanations will vary. Sample: I know because I looked at the first letters of each entry.
2. pages 20–23
3. the Gulf Stream
4. page 8
5. Answers will vary. Sample: No, this book does not discuss tsunamis. I can tell because there is no entry in the index for tsunamis.

Critical Thinking answers will vary. Sample: A book's index is in alphabetical order while a table of contents has things listed in the order in which they appear.

Index, p. 132

1. pages 12–15 and 28
2. Ida Tarbell
3. page 10
4. Answers will vary. Sample: Yes, the Gospel of Wealth is discussed. I know because it has an entry in the index.

Critical Thinking answers will vary. Sample: There is not an index in a fiction book because it is not full of facts and topics that readers would need to look up.

Glossary, p. 134

1. Answers will vary. Accept any two glossary terms.
2. Answers will vary. Student must write the definition for one of the two words listed in question #1.
3. Answers will vary. Sample: Acid rain has a high acid content due to pollution.
4. The word *aquatic* means "living in water."
5. Answers will vary. Sample: saber tooth tigers

Critical Thinking answers will vary. Sample: A glossary lists the meaning of important words used in the book but doesn't tell the page(s) on which the word is used.

Answer Key (cont.)

Glossary, p. 136

1. Answers will vary. Accept any two words from the glossary.
2. Answers will vary. Student must write the definition for the one of the words he or she listed in #1.
3. a hygrometer
4. Answers will vary. Sample: Most people like to live in a mild *climate* that is warm all year.

Critical Thinking answers will vary. Sample: I would use a glossary to look up the definition of a word in a nonfiction text if I couldn't figure out its meaning from context.

Contents of the Teacher Resource CD

Skill	Filename
Predict	
The Price to Play	page008.pdf page009.pdf
Double Crush	page010.pdf page011.pdf
Prior Knowledge	
Bird Watching	page012.pdf page013.pdf
Intruder in Gamba's Kingdom	page014.pdf page015.pdf
Set a Purpose	
The Heimlich Maneuver	page016.pdf page017.pdf
Mysteriously Mundane	page018.pdf page019.pdf
Ask Questions	
The Great Pacific Garbage Patch	page020.pdf page021.pdf
John Barry, Father of the American Navy	page022.pdf page023.pdf
Make Connections	
Alpine Competition	page024.pdf page025.pdf
Ski Cross	page026.pdf page027.pdf
Context Clues	
Birth of an Island	page028.pdf page029.pdf
Are Woolly Mammoths and Elephants the Same?	page030.pdf page031.pdf
Visualize	
My Noisy Alarm Clock	page032.pdf page033.pdf
Alexander the Great	page034.pdf page035.pdf
Conflict and Resolution	
Kenny Finds His Muse	page036.pdf page037.pdf
The Undead Chipmunks	page038.pdf page039.pdf

Skill	Filename
Characters	
The Eagle and the Kite	page040.pdf page041.pdf
The New Chess Player	page042.pdf page043.pdf
Literary Devices	
Memories from My Childhood	page044.pdf page045.pdf
The Waterspout	page046.pdf page047.pdf
Literary Themes	
Cruel Initiation	page048.pdf page049.pdf
Toss Me a Line!	page050.pdf page051.pdf
Title and Headings	
The U.S. Census Counts	page052.pdf page053.pdf
Leonardo da Vinci	page054.pdf page055.pdf
Typeface and Captions	
The First U.S. President	page056.pdf page057.pdf
The Interdependence of Life	page058.pdf page059.pdf
Graphics	
Community Newsletter	page060.pdf page061.pdf
Disease	page062.pdf page063.pdf
Topic Sentences	
The Vikings	page064.pdf page065.pdf
Florida	page066.pdf page067.pdf
Main Idea	
The Porpoise Trainer	page068.pdf page069.pdf
Let's Get Cooking!	page070.pdf page071.pdf

Contents of the Teacher Resource CD (cont.)

Skill	Filename
Details	
Blood Drive at Ellis JHS on January 18	page072.pdf page073.pdf
The Story That Caused an Uproar	page074.pdf page075.pdf
Main Idea and Details	
Domesticated Rats	page076.pdf page077.pdf
Falling Leaves	page078.pdf page079.pdf
Cousins and Best Friends	page080.pdf page081.pdf
Chronological Order	
Sally Ride	page082.pdf page083.pdf
Abigail Adams	page084.pdf page085.pdf
Logical Order	
Keep Your Eyes on the Prize	page086.pdf page087.pdf
Make Your Own Terrarium	page088.pdf page089.pdf
Fact and Opinion	
My New Grandfather	page090.pdf page091.pdf
Understanding Relative Humidity	page092.pdf page093.pdf
Proposition and Support	
Saving Our National Parks	page094.pdf page095.pdf
Fascinated by Space	page096.pdf page097.pdf
Author's Purpose	
Spay or Neuter Your Pet!	page098.pdf page099.pdf
Turning the Tide for Sea Turtles	page100.pdf page101.pdf
Compare and Contrast	
Choosing a College	page102.pdf page103.pdf
Making Electricity	page104.pdf page105.pdf

Skill	Filename
Cause and Effect	
Bad Boy Michaels Loses a Fan	page106.pdf page107.pdf
Amusement Park Rides	page108.pdf page109.pdf
Draw Conclusions	
Remember to Lock Up!	page110.pdf page111.pdf
Mohandas Gandhi	page112.pdf page113.pdf
Infer	
What Goes Up Must Come Down	page114.pdf page115.pdf
Accidental Discoveries	page116.pdf page117.pdf
Summarize	
Timing Races	page118.pdf page119.pdf
The Iroquois	page120.pdf page121.pdf
Paraphrase	
African History	page122.pdf page123.pdf
Azure Mist Saves the Day	page124.pdf page125.pdf
Table of Contents	
World Cultures Through Time	page126.pdf page127.pdf
India	page128.pdf page129.pdf
Index	
Storms	page130.pdf page131.pdf
Industrial Giants	page132.pdf page133.pdf
Glossary	
Inside Ecosystems	page134.pdf page135.pdf
Earth's Atmosphere	page136.pdf page137.pdf

Notes